MARKS ARE JUST NUMBERS

THE LEARNING MYTHS THAT SHAPED US
(AND WHY THEY'RE WRONG)

NAFEEZ AHAMED

Made with ❤ on the Notion Press Platform
www.notionpress.com

I dedicate this book to my three little wonders—my two little explorers and one brain-teaser, my son, who never stops asking questions. To my twin daughters, may your curiosity lead you to magical discoveries, and to my inquisitive son, may your endless questions light the way to understanding and creativity. This book is for you all, as you navigate the twists, turns, and infinite possibilities of life and learning.

And to all the students, past, present, and future, who feel lost in the maze of tests, grades, and societal pressures, this is for you. May you one day realize that real learning is not about the marks you score, but the knowledge and skills you gain along the way.

To all the parents, the ones who worry and wonder if their child is getting the right kind of education, this is for you as well. May you find comfort in knowing that education is not a race, but a journey—and it's okay to take your time to discover what truly matters.

This book is my humble offering to all those who seek something deeper, something more meaningful, in the world of learning. Here's to finding the real magic in education.

Contents

Contents

Introduction

If you've ever been handed a 97% report card only to be asked, "Beta, where did the 3 marks go?", this book is for you. If your parents called the neighbor's kid a "genius" because he scored half a mark more, this book is for you. If your idea of a thrilling childhood was memorizing multiplication tables, coaching center tests, and the crushing weight of your family's expectations —congratulations, you survived the Great Indian Education System!

For decades, we've collectively agreed that marks aren't just numbers—they're a currency of self-worth, family pride, and sometimes even your meal ticket to basic parental affection. Forget Disney; Indian childhoods come with their own villains: Rote Learning, Homework Monsters, and Aunty and Uncle Who Know Everything. And let's face it—if you haven't spent a Sunday afternoon justifying why you only got 95%, are you even Indian?

But here's where it gets serious (yes, this book has its moments). This isn't just a survival guide for students; it's an eye-opener for parents who are clueless about what real learning actually looks like. To all the aspiring parents out there: this book is your cheat sheet. Real education isn't about exam scores and report cards; it's about curiosity, creativity, and building skills that matter.

Spoiler alert: A child's success isn't measured in percentages but in their ability to think, question, and explore the world.

And to teachers—the unsung heroes who are caught between system-driven targets and the hopes of shaping young minds—this book is a love letter and a wake-up call. You play the most important role in transforming education into something meaningful. Let's not just create students who ace tests; let's inspire thinkers, creators, and problem-solvers who can survive—and thrive—in the real world.

Through humor, sarcasm, and some hard-hitting truths, this book unpacks the myths that plague our education system. Why does early memorization matter so much? Why do we think perfect English equals intelligence? And why is smart work still considered a shortcut while burning out is celebrated as dedication? We'll explore coaching centers that manufacture stress faster than results, parents who act like CEOs of "Project Child Success," and schools that value uniforms more than creativity.

This is not a book about rebellion—though you'll find plenty of reasons to question the present condition. It's about reclaiming childhood, redefining learning, and reimagining a system where curiosity is more important than competition. Because, let's face it: marks really are just numbers, and life is far too big to fit into a report card.

So, aspiring parents, dedicated teachers, and exhausted students, grab a cup of chai, tuck this book under your homework pile, and join us on a hilarious, insightful journey through the education system we know all too well. Let's learn, laugh, and remind ourselves that education isn't just about exams—it's about building a future that truly counts.

Preface

When I look back on my journey, I see a lifetime of learning—not just from books, but from experiences that shaped me as a student, a teacher, a principal, a trainer, and most importantly, a parent. This book is the culmination of those experiences, stretching from my days as a wide-eyed child in primary school to my current role as a parent navigating the education system for my 6-year-old son.

As a student, I learned to ace exams, but life taught me lessons that no textbook ever could. Those early years were all about marks, ranks, and rote memorization—tools that prepared me for exams but not for the real world. It was only later that I realized education is far more than the numbers on a report card.

For over a decade, I served as a teacher, and eventually, a principal. During those years, I witnessed firsthand the triumphs and trials of students, teachers, and parents. I saw the struggles of children burdened by unrealistic expectations, the frustrations of teachers bound by rigid syllabi, and the unwavering hope of parents striving to give their children the best.

The last five years have been transformative. As a trainer, I've traveled across South India, stepping into 350+ schools, training teachers, and working closely with students. These travels opened my eyes to the diverse ways schools function, how students learn, and what parents expect. Each school, each classroom, and each interaction has contributed to the insights shared in this book.

And then, there's my most personal journey—as the parent of a 6-year-old. In just two years, I've changed four schools, searching for the elusive "perfect" school that balances academics, life skills, and holistic development. That journey taught me that our education system often misses the mark when it comes to nurturing curiosity, creativity, and the ability to thrive in the real world.

This book is not just a critique of the system—it's a reflection of my journey and an exploration of what education could be. It's for students overwhelmed by expectations, teachers struggling to inspire beyond the syllabus, and parents navigating the chaotic world of report cards, coaching classes, and school admissions.

Through humor, reflection, and personal anecdotes, this book challenges myths that dominate our education system—from the obsession with marks to the sidelining of life skills. It asks tough questions: Are we preparing children for exams or for life? Are we nurturing thinkers, creators, and leaders—or just toppers?

I hope this book makes you laugh, think, and, most importantly, question the way we approach education. Because at the end of the day, learning isn't about marks—it's about growth, curiosity, and the ability to navigate life's challenges.

Here's to reimagining education—one page, one story, and one question at a time.

— Nafeez Ahamed

Acknowledgements

I begin this journey of gratitude with the first teacher I ever had—my mother. She taught me the basics of life, from how to walk and talk, to how to approach challenges with curiosity and resilience. It was in her gentle guidance that I learned the true meaning of love, patience, and perseverance.

As I ventured into the world of formal education, I encountered many more wonderful teachers whose influence has been nothing short of transformative. From my early school days to post-graduation, each teacher imparted more than just knowledge; they taught me how to think critically, how to question the status quo, and how to strive for excellence in everything I do. I owe my academic foundation to these educators who believed in me, even when I doubted myself.

I would also like to extend my heartfelt thanks to my friends, who introduced me to the real world beyond textbooks. Their experiences, perspectives, and insights have been invaluable in helping me shape my views on life and learning. Through them, I learned that true growth often happens outside the classroom.

The schools that I have had the privilege of working with have provided me the opportunity to dive deep into the education system, exploring both its strengths and areas for improvement. These experiences have been fundamental in shaping my understanding of how we can innovate and elevate the learning process.

To the students who have come across in my life—whether in the classroom or elsewhere—your enthusiasm, curiosity, and thirst for knowledge inspire me every day. You remind me of the immense potential within each of us, and your questions challenge me to rethink, learn, and grow.

I also owe a great deal of gratitude to the many people I've met in various roles at different places—each encounter has been an opportunity to broaden my horizons and deepen my understanding of the world. These interactions, whether brief or long-lasting, have shaped who I am today.

Finally, my deepest appreciation goes to my wife, whose unwavering support and belief in my ideas have been the cornerstone of my personal and professional life. Her encouragement has always been a driving force, motivating me to pursue my passions and take on challenges with confidence.

This journey has been shaped by the collective wisdom, experiences, and love of everyone mentioned here. To all those who have helped me along the way—thank you. You have played a crucial role in this chapter of my life, and I will always be grateful.

CHAPTER ONE

The Table-Memorizing Olympics

Welcome to the great Indian race to get your 5-year-old to memorize multiplication tables. Forget that the poor kid can barely count his fingers without missing one! Parents, fueled by WhatsApp wisdom and society's applause, believe their child's worth is tied to how fast they can chant, "2 times 2 is 4." But here's the kicker: <u>the education system doesn't recommend this at all,</u> and science says it's like teaching a toddler to sprint before they can walk.

"Rote learning might win exams, but understanding wins life."

Why This Myth is Practically Wrong

Your Child's Brain is Still in "Play Mode"
At 5, your child's brain isn't wired for abstract concepts like multiplication. They're better off counting toys or biscuits. By forcing rote memorization, you're teaching them words without meaning—like making them chant "aloo paratha" without knowing it's food.

No, They're Not Going to Become Einstein This Way
Memorizing tables doesn't make your child a genius; it makes them a parrot. Genius is born when kids *understand* concepts, like knowing multiplication is just adding the same number multiple times.

What Happens When They Grow Up?

Fast forward 15 years: Your child can recite tables backward but can't figure out how to split the bill at a restaurant or calculate discounts in a sale. Congratulations, you've raised a human calculator that only works when prompted!

What Works Best Instead: Let's Ditch the Memorization Madness

So, here we are, staring down the barrel of an education system that thinks the only way to success is by drilling multiplication tables into tiny, still-developing brains. But guess what? There's a much better way to teach your child math, and it doesn't involve flashcards or repetitive chanting. Here's the magical list of What Works Best Instead, served with a side of sarcasm. You're welcome.

Play-Based Learning: Because Kids Are Not Robots (Yet)

Who knew that children actually learn through play? Shocking, right? Turns out, forcing your child to memorize numbers isn't the best way to help them understand math. Instead, let them play! You know, the thing they do best. Building towers, playing with blocks, or running imaginary stores will teach them more about numbers than all the flashcards in the world. Who knew math could be learned while having fun? I know, it's a real revelation.

Real-Life Scenarios: Your Kid Doesn't Live in a Textbook

Forget abstract concepts like "6 times 4." Instead, let's talk about stuff they actually care about, like pizza. Yes, pizza. If we're splitting a pizza with 6 slices and each person gets 2, how many people are eating the pizza? This, my friend, is math that works. Real-life examples make math feel useful instead of some random fact that's about as relevant as memorizing the phone book.

Creative Expression: Math Isn't Just Numbers, It's Art (Apparently)

Ever tried combining art with math? Of course not, because why would you? But here's the twist: it works! Let your kid draw shapes, count them, and create patterns. It's not just a waste of crayons, it's math! "Let's draw 3 blue circles and 2 red squares, and now tell me how many shapes we have in total." Bingo! You're teaching them math through the sheer joy of creativity. Who knew?

Technology: The Kids Are Basically Already Part Computer

Oh, the horrors of screen time! Unless, of course, that screen is teaching your child math in an interactive, engaging way. Forget the outdated notion that screen time is ruining our kids' brains. In fact, when used wisely, apps and educational games can help kids learn math faster than any parent-prompted flashcard session. Gasp! Yes, a game on your phone might actually teach them more than you yelling at them to memorize 7 times 9. Who would have thought?

Group Learning: Because Who Doesn't Like a Little Peer Pressure?

Let's be real—kids are a lot more motivated when they can brag about how good they are at something. Enter group learning. Instead of torturing your child alone with multiplication tables, let them work in groups. They'll solve problems together, teach each other, and actually get math because they're having fun with their friends. Who needs solo misery when you can have group learning chaos and still come out ahead? Genius, really.

What to Look for in Schools:

When you look for a school, try to find one that focuses on understanding concepts rather than just memorizing them. A good school will help children understand why something works, instead of just making them memorize facts. For example, instead of forcing your child to memorize the multiplication tables, a school should teach them how multiplication works and how to use it in real-life situations. A great school will make learning fun and meaningful, so kids won't just repeat information—they'll understand it and be able to use it.

Let's Be Real—It's Time to Rethink Early Learning

So, maybe it's time we all calm down about early memorization. Instead of creating little human calculators, let's focus on helping kids actually understand math. Games, real-world examples, and letting them learn at their own pace can work wonders. Trust me, they'll eventually learn their times tables—and when they do, they'll actually know what to do with them. Until then, let them play, explore, and figure things out. Because life's too short to spend your childhood reciting 9 times 9.

Echoes of My Journey

Back in 10th standard, our math teacher had a foolproof strategy for us to score marks in the board exams. "Memorize the Pythagoras theorem," she declared, "because it's guaranteed to fetch you 5 marks!" And like obedient soldiers, we all lined up, reciting:

"In a right-angled triangle, the square of the hypotenuse is equal to the sum of the squares of the other two sides."

By the time of the exam, we could chant it in our sleep. Naturally, the question did come: "Prove the Pythagoras theorem." And just like parrots, the entire class scribbled the proof word-by-word, replete with the same diagrams, same equations, and even the same squiggly arrow marks.

5 marks secured! Glory day! The teacher was thrilled, the parents were proud, and the students? Well, we felt invincible. "We've mastered Pythagoras!" Or so we thought.

Fast forward five years. I'm sitting in a competitive exam hall, staring at a seemingly innocent question:

"A person starts at point A and walks 6 km to point B. From point B, the person takes a right-angle turn and walks 8 km to point C. Now, the person wants to know the shortest distance between point A and point C.
Can you calculate the distance between point A and point C?"

I froze. Somewhere deep in my subconscious, Pythagoras was screaming at me: "AC² = AB² + BC²!" But in that moment, I drew a complete blank. Not a single neuron fired to remind me of the theorem I'd so proudly memorized. Instead, I grabbed my pen and started drawing a scale on the paper, planning to measure the hypotenuse manually like some ancient cartographer solving a geometry puzzle.

Needless to say, I failed miserably. The realization hit me like a ton of bricks: What good is memorizing if you don't know how to apply it?

From that day, I made a silent promise to myself. Whenever I teach students, I'd never ask them to blindly memorize concepts. Instead, I'd ensure they understand them, see their practical applications, and learn to connect the dots.

And the results? My students can tell it better—those who've heard me constantly say, "Marks are Just Numbers," ensuring they prepare not just for exams, but for life.

CHAPTER TWO

Is Your Child a Student or a Full-Time Employee?

In the middle-class dream of private school education, there's one villain: **Homework**. Parents pay hefty fees so their kids can spend 5 hours at home copying textbook answers. Why? Because we've been conditioned to believe that "more homework = more success."

"Homework overload doesn't make your child a genius; it just makes them sleep-deprived zombies."

"Your child isn't your business plan. Let them thrive, not just survive."

Why This Myth is Practically Wrong

"*Quantity ≠ Quality*

Your child doesn't need 50 math problems to understand division. They need 5 good ones. Overloading them is like giving someone 20 plates of biryani when they only need one to feel full."

It's Killing Family Time

Instead of family dinners, we have homework crises: "Where's your English notebook? Why is your handwriting worse than a doctor's?" The evening ends in tears, not bonding.

Jobs Don't Work Like This

No office job requires you to write the same email 30 times. So why are we teaching kids this way? What they need is problem-solving skills, not endurance training for hand cramps.

Better Solutions :

1. **Practical Homework**
   Replace repetition with relevance. Instead of copying answers, ask them to observe something real: "What's the cost of 3 kg of rice? Find out."
2. **Limit Time**
   Homework shouldn't take more than 30 minutes to an hour. Let them have time to play, explore hobbies, or just stare at the ceiling—it's called creativity.
3. **Teach Independence**
   Help them only when absolutely necessary. Let them struggle a bit—it builds problem-solving skills. (Also, it saves you from turning into their personal assistant!)

Supporting Evidence: Finland's Got It Figured Out (While We're Still Drowning in Homework)

Let's talk about Finland, the golden child of education. Their system focuses on creativity, play, and collaborative learning, and guess what? They're killing it on global education rankings. Meanwhile, countries still drowning their kids in homework are scratching their heads, wondering why their students are burnt out and uninspired. Spoiler: It's the homework.

Research shows that kids in systems like Finland's—where play and creativity are prioritized over hours of rote homework—actually perform better academically. Turns out, when you let kids think critically and explore their interests, they thrive. Who knew?

So maybe it's time to take a hard look at our traditional "more homework equals more learning" philosophy. Because let's be real, when was the last time copying answers from the back of the book turned anyone into a problem-solving genius?

What to Look for in Schools:
When looking at schools, ask yourself, "How much homework does my child get, and is it useful?" A good school will assign homework that helps children understand what they're learning in class. For example, instead of giving long, boring worksheets, a school should give projects or activities that make the child think and apply what they've learned. If the homework is just busywork—like filling out pages and pages of questions without much thought—then it's not helping your child learn. You want a school that gives homework to reinforce learning, not just to keep your child busy. (**Note*** - <u>Projects or Activities doesn't mean sticking photos on paper, unless your child is in pre-school and neither it is copying from internet</u>)

What Parents Can Do to Impart Real Learning:
At home, it's important to help your child focus on the why and how of their homework, not just finish it quickly.

For example, if your child is given a math problem, help them think through it instead of just telling them the answer. Ask questions like, "How would you solve this problem in real life?" or "Can you explain why this step makes sense?" By helping your child understand the concepts and not just rush through the work, you're teaching them that learning isn't just about finishing assignments—it's about truly understanding what they're learning.

Conclusion: Let's Ditch the Homework Overload

"*Homework is not about quantity; it's about meaningful practice. Let's not turn children into overworked employees before they even hit puberty.*"

Here's the deal: we need to stop equating piles of homework with academic success. Instead of stressing kids out with tasks they're too exhausted to care about, let's give them room to breathe, think, and actually enjoy learning.

The future isn't about who spent the most hours hunched over their desk—it's about who can adapt, solve problems, and come up with creative ideas. So, let's rethink this whole homework obsession. More play, more creativity, and more time for kids to be, well, kids. Because life's too short to spend it doing math problems at 9 PM when all you really wanted was to watch cartoons.

Echoes of My Journey

Back in my primary school days, the most sacred ritual of our academic lives was homework. And not just any homework—no, we were given the glorious task of copywriting. Every evening, we'd receive our instructions:

"Copy this paragraph from your textbook 10 times to improve your handwriting."

As a young and obedient student (yes, I was once obedient), I followed this routine like clockwork. Day after day, week after week, I diligently copied the same text over and over, convinced that this tedious task was the key to academic success. But what did it really get me? A mountain of monotonous work and the sinking realization that no amount of copying would ever make me love handwriting—or any homework for that matter.

The result? Not only did my handwriting remain a mystery, but I also wasted countless hours mindlessly repeating the same lines, with no real understanding of the material. The textbooks didn't teach me anything new, and I never really got any better at what I was supposed to be learning. My brain, instead of absorbing information, was stuck in an endless loop of copying, like a hamster on a wheel.

Teachers, of course, kept saying, "Practice makes perfect!" But all it made was more mind-numbing repetition. The irony? Those hours of "practice" didn't help me master handwriting or the actual content. They just gave me the skill to finish homework without ever understanding what I was doing.

Now, as I reflect on it, I can't help but laugh at the sheer futility of it all. Wasn't there a better way to reinforce learning than wasting hours copying sentences that meant nothing? Why not engage in something creative, like writing about real-life experiences or exploring ideas that matter, rather than copying the same paragraph until your hand hurts?

So here's my advice: Homework shouldn't just be busywork. It should have purpose. Let's rethink how we approach learning. Because no matter how many times you copy "The quick brown fox jumps over the lazy dog," if you're anything like me, you'll just end up with a pile of work that taught you nothing. And that, my friends, is the real failure of homework.

CHAPTER THREE

Rulers, Threats, and Guilt Trips: The Indian Parenting Toolkit for Discipline

"Spare the rod and spoil the child" might just be the unofficial motto of Indian parenting. The middle-class struggle to give kids a better education often comes with a side dish of disciplinary practices straight out of a military boot camp. Parents assume that discipline requires punishment—scolding, slapping, or the dreaded "Wait till your father gets home."

But here's the truth: **"Punishment doesn't teach discipline; it teaches fear"**. And fear doesn't build a responsible adult—it builds an anxious one who dreads making mistakes.

Is it discipline or drama?

Why This Myth is Practically Wrong

> **"Fear ≠ Respect**
> *Making your child scared of you doesn't mean they respect you. It means they'll lie, hide, or avoid you when they make mistakes."*

Example: Your child spills water on their homework. Instead of asking for help, he hides the wet pages, hoping you won't see.

1. **Punishment Crushes Confidence**

Constant punishment sends the message: "You're not good enough." Over time, this can lead to low self-esteem and hesitancy to try new things.

Imagine a teenager afraid to join a debate team because "What if I mess up and everyone laughs?"—a fear planted by years of being scolded for minor mistakes.

2. It Doesn't Teach Responsibility

Punishment focuses on what *not* to do but rarely explains *why* something is wrong or how to do better.

Example: A child punished for coming home late learns to fear being late, not the importance of punctuality.

3. It's Outdated

The world has moved on from corporal punishment, but Indian homes and schools often cling to it like a relic of the British era. Modern psychology says positive reinforcement works better than threats and guilt trips.

Why Parents Need to Rethink This Practice

1. Your Child Isn't Your Stress Reliever

Middle-class parents juggling jobs, bills, and societal pressure often take out their frustrations on their kids. Remember: Your child didn't cause the traffic jam or your boss's bad mood.

2. Discipline is About Guidance, Not Control

The goal of discipline is to teach self-control and responsibility, not to create obedient robots.

3. Punishment Creates a Fear of Failure

Children who are punished harshly grow up avoiding risks because they associate mistakes with shame and pain. This mindset can limit their career and personal growth.

4. It's Unnecessary in a Changing World

In today's diverse career landscape, where professions range from wildlife photography to digital marketing, children need creativity and adaptability more than blind obedience.

Examples of Why the Myth Fails

1. **The Silent Rebel:**
   A child scolded for every mistake stops sharing their thoughts and feelings. By the time they're a teenager, they've mastered the art of secrecy, and parents are left wondering, "Why doesn't my child talk to me anymore?"
2. **The "Good Boy" Who Can't Say No:**
   Punished kids often become people-pleasers, unable to set boundaries. This adult ends up saying "yes" to overtime work, unnecessary favors, and even toxic relationships.
3. **The Career Dropout:**
   A child pushed into obedience might excel academically but fail to adapt when a career demands creativity, leadership, or independent thinking.

What Works Best Instead

1. **Positive Reinforcement**

Praise good behavior instead of only pointing out mistakes. Example: "You finished your homework on time—great job!"

Rewards can be simple: extra playtime, a favorite snack, or just a high-five.

2. Explain, Don't Threaten

If your child makes a mistake, calmly explain the consequences of their actions instead of yelling.

Example: "When you stay out late without telling me, I get worried. Next time, just let me know if you're going to be late."

3. Set Clear Rules and Consequences

Children thrive on structure. Make sure they know what's expected and what will happen if rules are broken.

Example: "If you don't finish your homework by 7 PM, you won't get screen time today."

4. Teach Problem-Solving

Help your child figure out how to fix their mistakes. Example: "You forgot your project at home. How can we make sure this doesn't happen again? Maybe we can create a checklist for your bag."

5. Be a Role Model

Children mimic what they see. If you handle stress with patience and calmness, they'll learn to do the same.

Why This Matters for Diverse Careers

- In professions like design, teaching, or event planning, creativity and problem-solving are key. Children raised with positive discipline are better equipped to handle challenges without fear.
- Disciplined yet confident adults thrive in roles like wildlife conservation, where quick decisions are needed, or journalism, where they must handle criticism gracefully.

Expert Opinions: Why Fear-Based Discipline Doesn't Work

Experts have long argued that fear-based discipline, like threats and punishment, doesn't teach children the right lessons. Dr. Barbara Coloroso, a renowned educator, suggests that when we punish children, we teach them to be afraid of us, rather than teaching them responsibility or how to make better choices.

Psychologists like Dr. Laura Markham emphasize the importance of positive discipline, where children are guided with understanding and support. When children are treated with respect, they are more likely to develop a sense of responsibility and self-control.

The Magic of "Good Job!"

Let's be real—kids thrive on positive reinforcement. You praise them for their good behavior, and suddenly they're little angels (well, most of the time). Studies back this up:

children raised with encouragement and kindness—not yelling and fear—are more likely to grow into emotionally balanced, self-disciplined adults.

Dr. John Gottman, an expert in emotional intelligence, basically says kids need warmth and guidance, not threats and guilt trips. The results? Better grades, healthier relationships, and higher self-worth. Sounds like a solid trade-off compared to, say, shouting them into temporary silence or making them cry over spilled milk (literally).

What to Look for in Schools:

If the school is using threats or guilt trips to get students to behave, you're in trouble. A good school fosters an environment of mutual respect. Discipline should never come from fear, but from understanding. Schools should teach kids the why behind the rules and give them the opportunity to reflect on their actions. If the school believes in punishing first and asking questions later, you might want to reconsider your options.

Conclusion: Let's Rethink Discipline

Here's the thing: fear might get you a quick "yes," but it won't help your kid figure out how to handle life. Sure, yelling or punishment might make them stop doing whatever annoying thing they're doing in the moment, but it won't teach them how to manage their emotions or solve problems down the line.

Instead of running a home like a boot camp, let's try something revolutionary—patience, empathy, and, dare I say, humor. Positive reinforcement doesn't mean you're raising spoiled brats; it means you're showing your kids how to think for themselves, own their mistakes, and do better next time.

So, next time your kid spills juice all over the couch, take a deep breath, crack a joke, and hand them a towel. Because teaching them how to handle life's messes is way better than just yelling about the mess. Bonus: they might even thank you for it one day. (Okay, maybe not until they're 30, but still.)

CHAPTER FOUR

The Parent Olympics: Where 'Comparison' is the Trophy, but the Kids Aren't Playing the Game!

Oh, the glorious sport of comparing children. Every parent has been there at some point, whether it's in a friendly conversation with another parent or during a family gathering where, let's face it, the competition is fierce.

Sharma Ji - "Well, Rohit is already reading Shakespeare at 5!"

Meanwhile, you're quietly trying to hide your 7-year-old's book - "How to Draw a Dinosaur".

Welcome to the ultimate parental Olympics, where the prize is just a tiny boost to your self-worth.

Now, before we get too deep, let's be clear: comparing your child to others is as useful as trying to compare a watermelon to a pineapple. They're both fruit, yes, but they're completely different. Yet, we do it. We do it all the time. We look at what others' children are doing and think, "Why isn't mine doing that?"

What better way to show love than comparing your child to everyone else's?

Why This Myth is Wrong

Every Child Is Different – Deal with It!

Yes, yes, we all know that children are unique snowflakes—each with their own rhythm, their own strengths, and their own learning curves. But do we really treat them that way? Of course not.

It's much easier to just look at little Aarav who can solve a Rubik's cube blindfolded and think, "Why doesn't my kid have that skill?"

Maybe your kid doesn't have a thing for color-coded cubes, but can build an entire Lego city without looking at the instructions. But does that get the same applause? Nope. Not even close.

We've been conditioned to look at the "achievements" on paper and forget about the real-world skills that make your child amazing.

The Test-Score Trap

Let's talk about grades. Oh, the beautiful, brutal system of comparing numbers.

"Aarav scored 98% in his Math test, and he's already memorized "*pi*" up to the 25th decimal place...!" And there you are, trying to remember if your kid even knows what pi is.

But here's the kicker—just because your child's test scores aren't at the top of the class doesn't mean they're any less talented. In fact, the kid who aces every test might be the same one who runs crying when asked to speak in front of the class, while your kid is standing up and giving a 10-minute talk on how dinosaurs probably tasted like chicken. Who's the real winner here?

Social Media, the Silent Villain

Oh, let's not even get started on social media. If you're not posting a picture of your kid reading a three-part novel in one sitting, are you even parenting?

Social media has turned us all into comparison junkies, as we scroll through post after post of "perfect" families and their "perfect" children.

"Look at Neha's daughter—she's 8 and she's already writing a novel on quantum physics!"

Meanwhile, your child is watching reruns of "Motu Patlu" and refusing to eat anything that isn't pizza.

We're all guilty of it. The pressure to match up is real. But let's face it—social media is a curated reality, not a reflection of your child's potential. Your kid's ability to tell an engaging bedtime story beats any picture-perfect study session any day.

The Real Solution: Stop Comparing, Start Celebrating Celebrate Your Child's Strengths

Stop trying to mold your child into someone else's version of "successful"—you know, like Sharma ji ka beta, who's already the CEO of a tech company at age 12.

Your child has their own unique personality, with their own journey. If they're not into building robots or solving math problems in their spare time, who cares?

Maybe they're a future chef who can create a delicious pasta from scratch, or an expert in gaming strategies, or a brilliant storyteller who can turn a grocery list into an epic tale. Instead of obsessing over what they should be doing based on someone else's child, focus on what they love and what they excel at. Celebrate that! Get them the kitchen gadgets, the gaming gear, or the notebook full of stories they need to pursue their passion.

Let them know that being true to themselves is far more important than being "Sharma ji ka beta." After all, comparing a fine-dining meal to a fast food combo doesn't make sense—both are great, just served differently.

Throw Out the "Perfect Child" Checklist

Seriously, where did we get this checklist from?

"My child should be speaking in full sentences at 18 months, reading at 3, and writing at 4. They should also be able to do advanced calculus by age 8 and have a YouTube channel by 10." Let's just stop.

Each child has their own pace, and that's perfectly okay. There's no one-size-fits-all when it comes to growth and development. Instead of measuring your child's worth by the milestones on someone else's list, create a checklist that's only about them. "Does my child enjoy what they're doing? Are they curious? Are they happy?" If you check those boxes, you're winning, no comparison needed.

Get Over the "Perfect Parent" Pressure

Here's a secret: no one has it all together.

Not the mom with the Pinterest-perfect home, not the dad who has his kid's entire extracurricular schedule planned out until they're 18. We're all winging it in some way.

Parenting isn't about keeping up with everyone else's version of success; it's about showing up for your kid, day after day. The truth is, no one else has a clue what's going on in your household. The kid who is excelling in school and is a star athlete may be secretly struggling with their own challenges. You'll never truly know someone's full story.

So, relax. Take a deep breath and enjoy the ride with your child, without constantly measuring it against the next person's version of perfection.

Conclusion

At the end of the day, comparing your child to others is like comparing apples to oranges—both are fruits, but they're entirely different.

Your child's unique journey is just that: theirs. Stop looking at what everyone else's child is doing and start focusing on what your child is passionate about.

And to all the parents who think their child is behind or doesn't measure up: <u>your child's timeline doesn't have to match anyone else's</u>. They're growing at their own pace, and trust me, they'll get to their destination just fine. And when they do? You'll be cheering the loudest, because it will have been their journey all along, not someone else's.

CHAPTER FIVE

Speak English or Be Left Behind: The Great Indian Fear

In middle-class India, there's a common belief that fluency in English is the ultimate marker of intelligence and success. Parents rush to enroll their kids in expensive English-medium schools, fearing that any deviation from Shakespearean fluency will doom them to a life of mediocrity. But here's the truth: While English is important in today's globalized world, it's not the *only* key to success. If it were, our grandparents—who managed in Hindi, Tamil, Kannada, or Bengali—would never have succeeded in anything!

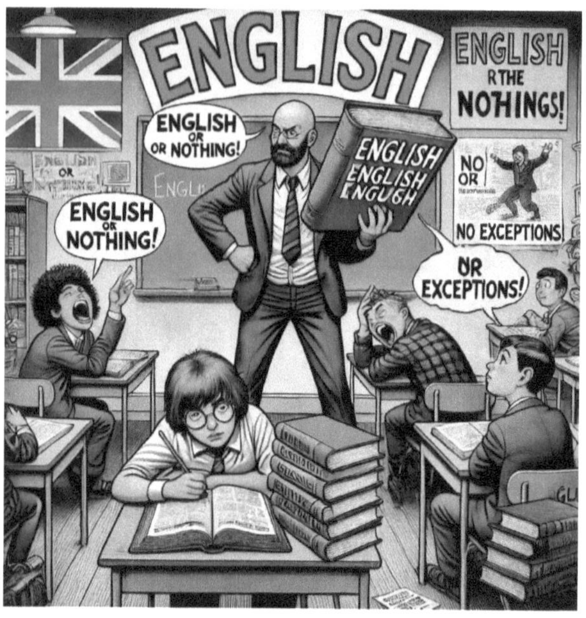

"Is language a tool for learning—or a barrier for growth?"

Why This Myth is Practically Wrong

1. Language Doesn't Equal Intelligence

Fluency in English doesn't make someone smarter. It simply means they're fluent in a language. Intelligence comes from problem-solving, creativity, and understanding concepts—none of which are tied to a specific language.

2. Lost Opportunities in Native Languages

In many professions, such as regional journalism, local politics, or rural healthcare, fluency in native languages is far more valuable than English. For instance, a Kannada-speaking social worker can connect better with rural communities than someone who speaks only English.

3. The Global Perspective

Countries like Japan, Germany, and France thrive economically without making English their primary language. They've proven that technical skills, innovation, and cultural pride matter more than the medium of communication.

4. Pressure Harms Kids

Forcing kids to "speak perfect English" from an early age creates anxiety and low self-esteem, especially for those who struggle with the language. Imagine being laughed at for mispronouncing a word—it stays with you for years.

Why Parents Need to Rethink This Practice

1. English Speaking is a Skill, Not a Status Symbol

Treat English as a tool, not a measure of success. A marketing executive fluent in Hindi or Tamil can still thrive with basic English proficiency if they're skilled at connecting with people.

2. Native Language Builds a Strong Foundation

Studies show that children learn better when taught in their mother tongue. Concepts like math, science, or social studies are easier to grasp when the child isn't struggling to understand the language itself.

3. No, the World Won't Judge Your Child

Parents often worry that speaking in their native language will make their child look "uncultured." The reality? Global professionals respect bilingual or multilingual individuals because they can communicate with diverse audiences.

4. Regional Careers Need Regional Languages

Many professions rely heavily on native language skills:

- **Lawyers** who draft contracts in local languages.
- **Tour guides** who explain cultural nuances to visitors.
- **Writers and poets** who preserve linguistic heritage.

What Works Best Instead

1. **Embrace Bilingualism**

Teach kids to be comfortable in both their native language and English. For instance, encourage them to use English at school but speak their mother tongue at home.

2. **Focus on Communication, Not Perfection**

"Whether your child says "Is" instead of "Are" doesn't matter as long as they communicate effectively. Remember, "grammar can be fixed, but confidence can't be rebuilt easily"."

3. Practical Language Learning

Encourage kids to learn languages in real-life contexts rather than through memorizing grammar rules. For example, practice English by reading storybooks, watching movies, or engaging in casual conversations.

Supporting Evidence

1. **UNESCO Studies on Mother-Tongue Education**

Studies by UNESCO show that children learn faster and perform better academically when taught in their mother tongue during foundational years.

2. **Economic Contributions of Regional Languages**

Regional industries like publishing, tourism, and local business rely heavily on native language skills, proving that success isn't tied to English alone.

3. Global Multilingual Success

Multilingual professionals are in high demand globally, especially in roles like diplomacy, international business, and translation services.

Conclusion

Parents, it's time to stop treating English as a status symbol and start valuing it as a skill. Encourage your child to master communication in *any* language, rather than obsessing over perfect English grammar. Whether your child becomes a regional storyteller, a global tech leader, or a tour guide in Varanasi, their language skills should empower them—not shackle them to societal expectations.

Echoes of My Journey

Back in the day, I was the proud student of an Urdu medium school until Grade 7. My relationship with English was limited to textbook words and a grudging respect for the alphabet. The only time I "spoke" English was during college programs, delivering memorized speeches with the confidence of a robot reading a script. I would rehearse them so much that even the punctuation marks seemed nervous.

Fast forward to today: I can confidently say that I now speak English far better than many of my English-medium counterparts, who've been learning it since they could toddle around in tiny uniforms. How? Not because I had fancy schools or started young, but because of one thing: a willingness to learn.

The funny part? While my friends from English-medium schools still fumble over words like entrepreneur and pneumonia, I can deliver entire conversations without breaking a sweat—and without ever having to memorize anything like those dreaded speeches!

The lesson here? It's not about when you start learning or which medium you study in—it's about your determination to improve. So, whether you're from an Urdu, Hindi, or English background, remember: willingness to learn will always outshine a fancy head start.

And hey, to my childhood self: if you're watching, we've come a long way from "Good morning, teachers and my dear friends"!

CHAPTER SIX

Born a Genius or Just Lucky? The Myth That Talent is Everything.

Oh, we've all heard it, right?

"some people are just born with a genius gene" - nonsense.

You know, the one where they claim someone's destined for greatness because they apparently came out of the womb already solving algebraic equations faster than you can say "Pythagorean theorem." But how much of that so-called "genius" is actually hardwired at birth?, and how much is the result of hard work?, learning from failures, and sheer persistence?

From the moment we hear about someone exceptional, the assumption is often the same: they must have been born with it. But let's pause and ask ourselves: Can talent alone truly explain success? Or is it the quiet, relentless grind of growth that shapes the path to greatness?

It's time to rethink what it means to be a genius—and whether we can all cultivate our own brand of brilliance, regardless of where we start.

"Is talent a gift, or just hard work in disguise? Debunking the myth that genius is born, not made."

Why This Myth is Practically Wrong

1. Talent Without Effort is Useless

Even the most gifted child will crash and burn if they don't put in the effort. A naturally good cricketer won't go anywhere without training, practice, and—dare I say it—consistency.

Example: Virat Kohli might have had raw talent, but it's his years of relentless practice that transformed him into a global icon. Talent didn't do that—he did.

2. Consistency Beats Talent Every Time

You know those so-called "average" kids who somehow always outshine the naturally talented ones? They work harder. Simple as that. Consistency builds skills, and skills often beat pure talent.

Example: A child who sketches every day, even though they're not a "born artist," will eventually surpass the kid who's naturally gifted but never picks up a pencil.

3. Talent is Just the Starting Point

Think of talent as a spark. It's cute. But unless you add fuel, it's just... well, a spark. Without consistency, even the brightest spark will fizzle out.

Example: A student with a knack for writing won't become a bestselling author unless they sit down, write, revise, and learn the craft. The trick? They won't get far just waiting for inspiration to strike. They'll need effort, the real key ingredient.

4. It Ignores the Role of Passion

Passion often trumps talent. A child passionate about photography, even without "natural talent," can still become a great photographer through practice, learning, and experimenting—you know, the stuff that takes time.

<u>Why Parents Need to Rethink This Practice</u>
1. Your Child Doesn't Need to Be a Prodigy

Most successful people weren't "child prodigies." They discovered their interests, worked on their skills, and succeeded over time.

2. Failure is Not a Verdict

Struggling at first doesn't mean your child isn't "meant" for something. Every beginner struggles—success comes to those who persist.

Example: A child who initially struggles with swimming might eventually win medals after consistent effort and good coaching. It's not about talent—it's about working smarter.

3. It's Not a Competition

Parents love comparing their kids to others: "Sharma ji's daughter paints so well, but mine can't even draw a straight line." This mindset discourages children and creates unnecessary pressure. Let them figure things out at their pace and, heck, let them enjoy the process. You know, smart work—without the stress.

<u>Examples of Why the Myth Fails</u>
The "Naturally Smart" Child Who Fails

A child who coasts through school without much effort often crashes and burns when faced with tougher challenges because they never learned how to work smarter. So much for that "natural" intelligence.

The Late Bloomer

A student who showed no early signs of talent in public speaking but practiced over the years becomes a charismatic leader in their company. Funny how effort trumps "natural" ability every time.

The "Jack of All Trades" Misjudgment

A child curious about everything—drawing, writing, coding—is often labeled as "unfocused." But this variety is a blessing. Their ability to adapt and tackle new challenges with smart strategies is exactly what helps them discover their true passion later.

<u>What Works Best Instead</u>
Focus on Effort, Not Labels

Praise your child's smart work rather than labeling them as "talented" or "not talented." Example: "I'm proud of how much time you spent practicing that song!" This builds smart work habits.

Encourage Exploration

Let your child try different activities without expecting immediate results. They might find a hidden passion or skill they didn't even know they had. Smart work means exploring without pressure.

Teach a Growth Mindset

Help your child understand that skills can be developed with consistent effort. Reinforce the idea that **"not yet" doesn't mean "never."** It's about getting better by learning from mistakes—without that over-hyped "gifted" label.

Provide Resources and Opportunities

Give your child access to tools, classes, or mentors to help them improve. For example, if they're interested in photography, invest in a basic camera and guide them to free online tutorials. Because smart work often involves using the right resources, not just hoping they're born with it.

Be Patient

Progress takes time. Instead of demanding overnight results, encourage steady improvement. A "quick fix" mentality won't help anyone build the necessary skills for long-term success.

Expert Opinions: Talent Is Only Part of the Equation

Experts like Dr. Carol Dweck, known for her work on mindset, emphasize that talent is only a small part of the equation. While natural abilities can give a child a head start, it's persistence, smart work, and the right mindset that lead to true success. Dr. Dweck's research shows that children who believe they can grow and improve through effort—rather than relying solely on their innate talent—are more likely to succeed in the long run. This is why fostering a growth mindset is key to unlocking a child's potential.

Supporting Evidence:
Research on the 10,000-Hour Rule
Malcolm Gladwell popularized the idea that mastery requires 10,000 hours of practice. This applies to musicians, athletes, and even professions like coding or marketing. You don't get better by relying on talent alone—you get better by putting in the work.

Educational Psychology
Studies show that praising effort instead of innate ability helps children develop resilience and a willingness to take on challenges. Because when you teach your child to rely on smart work rather than waiting for magic to strike, they'll thrive.

Conclusion: A Better Way Forward
It's time to stop treating talent like it's some magical superpower that guarantees success. Let's be real—natural talent can only take you so far. What really matters is effort, consistency, and the ability to learn from mistakes (because, everyone makes them). Instead of obsessing over how "gifted" a kid is, how about we focus on teaching them the value of smart work and a growth mindset? You know,

that thing where they realize they're not stuck with the skills they're born with—they can actually get better at stuff by trying. Shocking, I know.

Success isn't about being born with a silver spoon or a genius-level IQ. It's about rolling up your sleeves, putting in the work, and figuring out how to bounce back when life throws curveballs. So, let's stop telling kids they're "naturally gifted" and start showing them that grit, resilience, and a willingness to fail (and try again) are the real superpowers. Talent is nice, sure, but smart work is what turns it into something worth celebrating.

CHAPTER SEVEN

Screens, Gadgets, and Panic Attacks: The Great Technology Debate.

Technology in education is like a double-edged sword—on one side, there's the thrill of online classes, educational apps, and coding workshops promising to turn your child into the next tech prodigy.

On the other, there's the nightmare of endless screen time and your child knowing more about YouTube than anything resembling actual schoolwork.

Technology is either hailed as a miracle or blamed as a huge distraction. But here's the truth: when used correctly, technology is just a tool, not a replacement for learning. So, maybe it's time to stop pointing fingers at screens and start learning how to use them properly. Surprising, huh?

"Sometimes, the best lessons come with popcorn. Education beyond the classroom."

<u>Why This Myth is Practically Wrong</u>

1. Not All Screen Time is Bad

There's a difference between binge-watching cartoons and exploring a science experiment on YouTube. The key is to monitor *how* technology is being used.

Example: Watching videos about ancient civilizations can be as educational as reading about them in textbooks, especially for visual learners.

2. Overuse Can Be Harmful

When used excessively or without structure, technology can lead to reduced attention spans and unhealthy habits. But <u>blaming technology alone is like blaming a stove for a burnt dish</u>—it's all about how you use it.

3. It's a Skill, Not a Luxury

In today's world, tech skills are as important as reading or writing. Jobs in graphic design, data analysis, programming, and even marketing rely heavily on technology. Denying kids access to tech tools is like teaching them to swim without water.

<u>Why Parents Need to Rethink This Practice</u>

1. It's Not the Enemy

Technology isn't here to ruin childhoods. It's here to make learning more accessible, interactive, and fun.

Example: A child interested in astronomy can use apps to stargaze and learn about constellations—something no textbook can replicate.

2. Moderation is Key

Instead of banning gadgets outright, focus on creating healthy habits. For instance, limit screen time to educational activities during the week and recreational use on weekends.

3. The Future is Digital

From marketing to architecture to medicine, almost every profession today requires some level of tech proficiency. Preparing your child for the future means embracing technology, not avoiding it.

4. It's Affordable, Too

Middle-class parents often worry that technology is expensive. But many resources—like Khan Academy, YouTube tutorials, and coding platforms—are free or very affordable.

Examples of Why the Myth Fails

1. The "All or Nothing" Parent:

Parents who ban gadgets entirely often find their kids sneaking screen time without supervision. These kids end up using tech unproductively because they're not taught how to use it responsibly.

2. The Overloaded Child:

On the flip side, a child allowed unlimited screen time might learn a lot about Minecraft but very little about anything else.

3. The Late Bloomer in Tech Skills:

A student who avoids technology entirely may struggle later in college or the workplace, where tech literacy is essential.

What Works Best Instead

1. Set Clear Boundaries

Create a routine where tech use is balanced with physical activity, hobbies, and family time. For example:

- Weekdays: 1 hour of educational screen time.
- Weekends: 2 hours of recreational screen time.

2. Use Tech for Active Learning

Encourage activities that require interaction, like coding projects, online quizzes, or creating videos. Passive consumption (like endless scrolling) should be minimized.

3. Encourage Collaboration

Use technology to connect kids with peers for group learning. For example, they can collaborate on a project using Google Docs or join a virtual book club.

4. Teach Digital Responsibility

Teach your child to use technology safely and responsibly, from avoiding online scams to understanding the importance of digital privacy.

5. Introduce Diverse Tools

Introduce your child to a variety of tech-based learning tools based on their interests:

- **Curious about science?** Try apps like NASA's Eyes on the Solar System.
- **Interested in art?** Explore digital painting software like Krita.
- **Loves games?** Introduce them to educational platforms like Minecraft: Education Edition.

Supporting Evidence

1. Blended Learning Success

Research shows that a combination of traditional teaching and tech-based tools improves learning outcomes. Students who learn through interactive apps or videos often retain information better.

2. Global Best Practices

Countries like Singapore integrate technology into education from an early age, teaching kids coding, robotics, and digital literacy alongside traditional subjects.

3. Affordability and Accessibility

Online platforms offer quality education at a fraction of the cost of traditional coaching classes, making advanced learning accessible to middle-class families.

Conclusion: Stop Blaming Screens—Start Using Them Wisely

Let's stop treating technology like it's Thanos. Screens aren't the enemy; misuse is. Instead of banning devices, let's teach kids how to use them responsibly and creatively. Show them that tech isn't just for doom-scrolling and gaming—it's a gateway to learning, exploration, and building real-world skills.

The goal isn't to throw screens out the window; it's to make sure they're adding to a child's life, not taking over. Teach them balance: use screens to learn, then go outside and kick a ball. That's how we prepare them for a world where technology is everywhere. Because, let's be real, you can't ban tech—it's already here to stay. So, why not make it work for us?

CHAPTER EIGHT

Hard Work or Smart Work: Which One Really Gets You Ahead?

Ah, the myth that's been passed down through generations: **Hard work = Success.** But let's be honest, if that were true, then we'd all be walking around with Nobel Prizes, and the world would be full of genius gardeners and philosophical traffic policemen. The truth is, while hard work is important, it's not the **only** ingredient in the success recipe. In fact, if you're only relying on hard work without any smart strategies, you're like a dog chasing its own tail: you're busy, but you're going nowhere.

"The same goal, two different journeys. Which path would you choose?"

"*Here's the math:*
Hard Work *(endless hours of toil)* + **No Strategy** *(because, who needs one?)* = **Burnout, Exhaustion, and Zero Innovation.**"

Smart work, on the other hand, is like using a calculator when solving algebraic equations—you can still work hard, but you don't have to spend 20 minutes doing something that could be done in 5 seconds. So let's stop pretending that spending every waking hour buried in textbooks makes you a success story. Instead, let's talk about working smart and **getting ahead**.

Why This Myth is Wrong

1. The "More Hours, More Results" Myth
It's the ultimate educational trap: the more hours you spend in front of your books, the better your grades will be. Wow,

what a revolutionary concept!

Here's the catch—spending hours reading the same page over and over again doesn't magically turn you into Einstein. If that were true, the library would be full of geniuses who never went outside.

But guess what? More hours does **not** equal more learning. In fact, it might even be the opposite. It's like trying to fill a bathtub with a teaspoon. You're working hard, but you're getting nowhere.

Smart work is about focusing on the right things and using the most effective methods. So stop turning your life into a marathon of memorization.

2. The Myth of the 'Ideal' Hard Worker

We've all been there, right? The overachiever who brags about working day and night, burning the candle at both ends, and drinking way too much coffee. Meanwhile, they haven't made a single meaningful breakthrough.

The truth is, the "ideal" hard worker is often the one stuck in the details, constantly busy with tasks but never stepping back to see the big picture. The best workers don't drown in the grind—they know how to step back, assess, and **use their brain**. That's where the real productivity happens.

Better Solutions: Working Smart (For Students)

Use the Right Tools

Still trying to memorize every single fact for that history test? Come on, you're not auditioning for a brainiac competition.

Use some smart tools! There are apps that give you flashcards, study guides, and even quizzes to help you study better, faster, and without pulling out your hair.

Technology is your friend—use it to make studying easier, not harder. Trying to remember every little detail in a textbook is overrated. Let the apps do the heavy lifting while you focus on what really matters.

Prioritize and Delegate

Here's the thing: not all tasks are created equal. That essay on why penguins are the cutest animals? It's important, but so is that math assignment you've been putting off. The key is to prioritize your time wisely.

Tackle the tougher tasks first, then breeze through the easier ones. And remember, teamwork is key—group projects aren't about doing everything yourself. Assign tasks, split the work, and make the most of your time. The goal isn't to show off how much you can juggle—it's to get things done efficiently.

Take Breaks, They're Not the Enemy

Let's be honest, if you're trying to study for hours straight without a break, you're just setting yourself up for a mental meltdown. Taking breaks isn't cheating—it's science.

Your brain can only focus for so long before it needs to recharge. So, instead of powering through and zoning out halfway through your study session, take a short break. Walk around, stretch, grab a snack—whatever helps you refresh.

Your productivity will skyrocket, and you'll remember more than if you just forced yourself to keep going. Trust me, your brain will thank you.

Learn the Art of Saying No

We all know the overachiever who says yes to every club meeting, every last-minute group project, and every single party invite. You? You're smarter than that.

Saying yes to everything just means you're spreading yourself too thin, and let's face it, you're not a superhero. Focus on the tasks that actually matter to you and your goals.

Saying no is a superpower, and you've got it! Protect your time like it's the last slice of pizza—you don't owe anyone an explanation for taking care of yourself.

What to Look for in Schools:
So, does the school believe that working hard means working yourself into exhaustion, or do they encourage working smart—balancing effort with efficiency?

You want a school that teaches kids to solve problems, think critically, and use their brains, not just grind away mindlessly. It's not about staying up late doing endless assignments—it's about figuring out the best way to work, solve problems, and be productive. Ask: "Does the school encourage creative solutions, or are they stuck in the 'just work harder' mindset?"

What Parents Can Do to Help at Home:
Parents, let's be real—life's too short to work yourself into the ground. Teach your kids that it's not just about how hard they work, but how they work smart. Help them plan their tasks, manage their time, and focus on working efficiently.

Instead of pushing them to just do more and more, teach them how to prioritize. For example, when your kid is overwhelmed with homework, sit down with them and help them figure out which tasks need the most attention first. This way, they'll learn that success isn't about how many hours you put in, but about how you approach problems.

Conclusion

So, let's get real. Working hard is important, but it's not the whole equation. If you're working hard but getting nowhere, maybe it's time to rethink your strategy. <u>Smart work isn't about working less—it's about working efficiently</u>. It's about using the right tools, being strategic, and not falling into the trap of "more hours = better results."

So next time someone brags about how many hours they've spent studying, you can just smile and say, "That's great, but I've been working smart. Let's see who gets ahead." And spoiler: It'll probably be you.

CHAPTER NINE

The Bright Student vs. The Dull Student: Is There Really a Difference?

Ah, the classic equation we've all been taught:

"Bright Student = Success and Dull Student = The Struggle Bus."

If you're anything like me, you've probably spent years thinking that being a "bright" student meant you're on the fast track to greatness, while being "dull" meant you might as well be in a slow-motion replay of life, moving at the pace of a snail on a lazy Sunday. But hold on—let's break this down, shall we?

Just because someone excels at memorizing a bunch of facts doesn't mean they're the next big thing in the world of innovation.

On the flip side, the "dull" student might just be the next Einstein in disguise, hiding under a pile of misunderstood potential and possibly a mountain of unfinished homework.

"Labels don't define potential. Every student shines when given the right light."

Let's see how these numbers actually work out:

"Bright Student = Good Grades + Natural Talent + A Little Luck
Dull Student = Misunderstood Learning Style + Lack of Interest + A Really Bad Teacher"

So, can we please stop pretending that being labeled "bright" is the ultimate achievement? It's time to realize that **bright** and **dull** aren't labels, they're just variables in a much bigger equation called **personal growth**.

Why This Myth is Wrong

Intelligence Is Not a Fixed Asset

The myth of the "bright" student assumes that intelligence is something you're born with. "Oh, Reena, she's just so smart. She gets everything on the first try." Sure, Reena is great at acing tests, but can Reena build a functioning rocket ship out of paperclips? Probably not.

<u>The truth is, intelligence isn't something you either have or don't have. It's something that grows with practice, failure, and determination.</u> It's not about how quickly you can memorize a formula; it's about how well you can solve problems and think critically.

Let's stop pretending that being "bright" means automatically winning at life. And yes, there are many 'so called' dull students who end up being the ones who change the world—just ask Steve Jobs.

Grades Don't Define Potential

"

<u>Grades are like the likes on an Instagram post</u>. Sure, they give a sense of popularity, but they don't actually tell you if someone's really making a difference in the world. "

The so called-"bright" students are often those who can memorize information with ease, but that doesn't mean they've got the creativity, problem-solving skills, or passion that will drive innovation.

Schools and society need to stop measuring potential by the number of A's you have and start considering what you're capable of outside the classroom.

'So Called' Dull students often think in different, more creative ways, but if they're forced to comply to the rigid educational system, they end up being labeled as "slow." Remember, Albert Einstein was famously told by his teacher that he would "never amount to anything." Funny how that turned out, right?

The "Perfect Student" Is a Myth

There's this glorification of the "perfect student" who doesn't mess up, who always gets straight A's, and who seems like a walking, talking textbook. But guess what? Even the "perfect" student is probably afraid to take risks and make mistakes. Why? Because they're terrified of failing and losing their "bright" label.

> "*The truth is;*
>
> *Best students are those who **dare to fail**, dare to try things that are outside the textbook, and dare to ask questions that nobody else dares to ask.*"

A "dull" student may just be the one who experiments and learns by doing, rather than memorizing, and those are the qualities that will matter in the long run.

Better Solutions: Redefine What It Means to Be a "Good Student"

Encourage Diverse Learning Styles

Let's face it: not every student learns the same way. Some people <u>learn by doing</u>, others <u>by listening</u>, and others <u>by reading</u>. The system, however, often expects students to all be able to sit still and memorize a textbook, regardless of how they actually learn best.

Schools should embrace diverse learning styles. Maybe the "dull" student is really a hands-on learner who just needs a bit of practice with the material. Instead of focusing on one standard method of learning, schools should provide opportunities for different kinds of learners to shine. Encourage creativity, exploration, and independent thought. Every student can be a **bright** student when given the chance to learn in their own way.

Shift the Focus from Grades to Skills

Grades should not be the measure of a student's worth. We need to shift the focus away from "Who got the highest marks?" to "Who learned the most?" or "Who can apply what they've learned to real-world problems?"

Encourage students to focus on developing critical life skills like communication, teamwork, and problem-solving. These skills are far more important than memorizing the periodic table.

Celebrate Effort, Not Just Results

We need to encourage a growth mindset in schools. Let's celebrate effort, improvement, and persistence, rather than just celebrating natural talent or perfect scores. The student who's struggled through a difficult subject but never gave up is just as valuable, if not more than the student who aced the test without breaking a sweat. By celebrating effort, we'll create a school culture that fosters resilience and curiosity, rather than one that punishes failure and rewards perfectionism.

Foster Curiosity and Experimentation

Instead of just testing how well students memorize information, schools should encourage students to **ask questions** and **experiment**.

The "dull" student might be the one who asks questions that nobody else has thought of, or they might find new ways of solving a problem. The goal isn't to have a room full of robots who can only answer textbook questions—it's to have a room full of critical thinkers and problem solvers.

Let's focus on creating an environment where students feel comfortable experimenting, failing, and learning from their mistakes.

The Damage of Labels: Why 'Dull' Isn't a True Reflection?

Let's talk about the damage done when a student is labeled as "dull." We all know how easy it is for teachers, parents, and even peers to slap that label on a kid who's struggling in class. But here's the thing: that label isn't just a word—it's like a mental weight that drags the student down.

Imagine being told over and over again that you're "slow" or "dull." What do you think happens? That kid starts believing it. They start thinking they're just not as smart as the others, and suddenly, they stop trying. Why bother, right? If you're already "dull," what's the point of putting in the effort? It's like being handed a roadblock before you even get started.

This negative self-image becomes their new reality, and it doesn't matter how many opportunities they get or how much potential they have—it's buried under layers of self-doubt and a fear of failure. The kid isn't "dull" at all; they're just trying to figure things out in their own time.

The real tragedy is that the more we focus on that label, the less we allow them to see what they're truly capable of. So, maybe it's time to ditch the labels and start seeing kids for who they are—unique individuals with their own pace and path to success.

Alternatives to Labeling Students as "Dull"

Instead of labeling students as "dull," which carries a negative connotation and undermines their potential, schools should focus on identifying and celebrating each student's unique strengths and learning styles. For example, instead of calling someone **"dull,"** why not refer to them as a **"visual learner," "hands-on learner," or "problem solver"?** These labels acknowledge that students may excel in ways that aren't immediately reflected in traditional tests.

You could also use terms like **"creative thinker," "explorer," or "innovator"** to describe students who may not excel in the usual academic measures but show exceptional promise in other areas. This helps foster a more inclusive and positive learning environment where every student feels valued for their individuality, rather than boxed into a one-size-fits-all category. It's time to replace the term "dull" with something more empowering, like **"a work in progress"** or **"a future problem solver,"** because in reality, every student has the potential to shine.

Supporting Evidence: The Impact of Labels on Student Performance

Research shows that labeling students as "bright" or "dull" can have a profound impact on their performance. A study from Princeton University found that students who were labeled as "gifted" performed better than those labeled as "average," even if the students in both groups had the same academic ability.

Reason? The "gifted" students were more motivated to work hard, while the "average" students often felt discouraged and underperformed. This evidence shows that labels can limit a student's potential, while a focus on growth and improvement encourages greater success.

What Parents Can Do to Help at Home:

As a parent, stop comparing your child to others, and for heaven's sake, stop calling them "dull" just because they don't get straight A's. Every child learns differently. Help them embrace their unique learning style. If they're struggling, don't freak out; instead, give them strategies to work through problems and learn at their own pace. Encourage them to stick with it, even when things get tough. Praise effort, not just results. That way, you'll raise a child who values persistence and growth over "natural talent." Spoiler alert: perseverance wins in the end.

Conclusion: A Better Way Forward

It's time to stop labeling children as "bright" or "dull." Instead, let's focus on helping them grow and improve through effort, persistence, and support. Every child has the potential to develop their skills and reach their goals, no matter where they start. By fostering a growth mindset and encouraging kids to embrace challenges, we can help them unlock their full potential. After all, success isn't about being born with talent—it's about being willing to put in the work and learn from your experiences.

CHAPTER TEN

If It's Not on the Report Card, Does It Even Matter?

For middle-class parents, academics often feel like the center of the universe. Everything else—sports, art, music, dance—is just a "time pass."

The myth here is that extracurricular activities and life skills are distractions from a child's real goal: good grades.

But here's the truth: Academics will teach your child to solve equations, but life skills and extracurriculars will teach them how to solve life's challenges. So, unless you plan to hire a tutor to handle every real-world problem for them, it's time to rethink what success really means.

"What would you rather master: equations or empathy, diagrams or decision-making?"

1.   Life Skills Are Essential for Any Job

Regardless of whether your child becomes an engineer, teacher, artist, or entrepreneur, they'll need skills like teamwork, communication, time management, and adaptability.

Example: A programmer who can't collaborate with their team will struggle, no matter how well they code.

2. Extracurriculars Build Confidence

Activities like debate, sports, or drama help children develop self-confidence and public speaking skills, which are critical for professional success.

Example: A shy student who joins a debate club learns to articulate their thoughts and handle criticism—skills that will serve them in job interviews and beyond.

3. Academics Alone Don't Define Success

A good report card might land your child a job interview, but life skills and extracurricular achievements will help them ace it. Employers value creativity, leadership, and problem-solving, none of which are taught in textbooks exercises.

4. Hobbies Are Stress Busters

In a world full of deadlines and pressure, hobbies provide a much-needed outlet for stress and improve mental health.

Why Parents Need to Rethink This Practice

1. Life Isn't a Classroom

While academic knowledge is important, real-life challenges—like managing finances, handling failures, or negotiating—aren't found in textbooks.

2. Jobs Are Changing

Today's job market values well-rounded individuals. Fields like event management, digital marketing, and social media content creation demand a mix of creativity, adaptability, and communication skills.

3. Diverse Skills Open Doors

Extracurriculars often introduce children to new interests and career paths. A child passionate about dance might explore choreography, while a chess enthusiast might develop strategic thinking useful in business.

4. Not Everything is Measured in Marks

Creativity, resilience, and leadership can't be graded, but they're the foundation of success in any field.

Examples of Why the Myth Fails

1. The One-Dimensional Topper:

A student with excellent grades but no interpersonal skills struggles in group discussions or client-facing roles.

2. The Multi-Talented Achiever:

A child who balances academics with sports learns time management, builds confidence, and often excels in both areas.

3. **The Hobby Turned Career:**

A child who starts painting as a hobby might discover a career in graphic design, proving that "time pass" can lead to success.

What Works Best Instead

1. **Prioritize Balance**

Encourage children to balance academics with one or two extracurricular activities.

Example: Let them spend weekends playing cricket or learning an instrument, ensuring they still have time for studies.

2. **Focus on Skills, Not Just Grades**

Teach life skills like cooking, budgeting, and decision-making alongside academics.

Example: Involve them in planning the monthly grocery budget to teach financial literacy.

3. **Let Them Choose**

Allow your child to pick activities they genuinely enjoy. Forcing them into sports or music they dislike defeats the purpose.

4. Celebrate Non-Academic Achievements

Whether your child wins a debate competition, scores a goal in football, or completes a DIY project, celebrate their efforts as much as you would academic success.

5. Incorporate Skills into Daily Life

Use everyday situations to teach problem-solving, negotiation, and communication.

Example: If your child wants a new toy, ask them to research prices, compare options, and present their case—life skills in action!

Supporting Evidence

1. Global Trends in Education

Finland's education system, one of the best in the world, emphasizes extracurricular activities and life skills alongside academics, producing well-rounded, successful individuals.

2. Research on Extracurriculars

Studies show that students involved in extracurricular activities perform better academically and develop stronger leadership and teamwork skills.

3. Corporate Expectations

Employers increasingly value soft skills like communication and adaptability, often asking about extracurriculars in interviews to gauge these traits.

Expert Opinions: The Importance of Life Skills

Experts like Dr. Howard Gardner, the creator of the theory of multiple intelligences, argue that academic success is only one piece of the puzzle. In his view, skills like interpersonal intelligence, creativity, and emotional regulation are just as important, if not more so, for success in life. Schools that focus solely on academic performance often overlook these essential life skills, which are crucial for both personal happiness and professional success. Dr. Gardner suggests that an education system should value these other intelligences just as much as traditional academic ones.

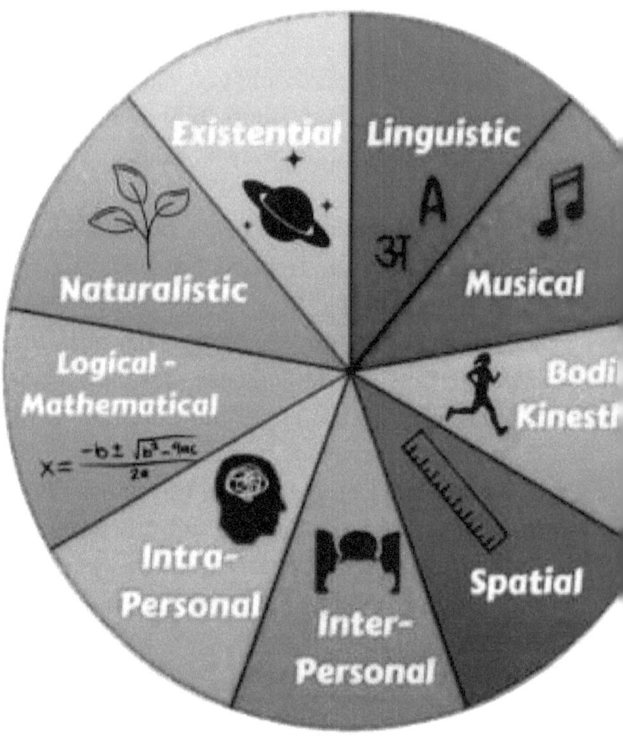

Multiple Intelligence - Howard Gardner

Conclusion

Parents, it's time to retire the myth that only academics matter. Success in life isn't about knowing all the capitals of the world—it's about being resourceful, creative, and resilient. Let your child explore their passions, build essential life skills, and develop into a well-rounded individual. After all, the best report card is the one that prepares them for life, not just exams.

CHAPTER ELEVEN

The Forgotten Classroom: Why Sports Matter More Than We Think

Ah, sports—the subject that gets a 'zero period' in the timetable but somehow manages to teach more life lessons than any textbook. Let's face it: every student has been told at least once, 'Focus on your studies, Football can wait!' Meanwhile, the only thing football is waiting for is to teach your child teamwork, resilience, and how to lose with grace.

.When balancing textbooks and football feels like a full-time job.

The Myth That Sports Are Just a Distraction

Yes, you heard it right. Sports, the so-called 'distraction' that teaches everything from teamwork to handling defeat, but apparently, it's not nearly as important as memorizing the periodic table for the 87th time. After all, when was the last time your child came home crying because they didn't score enough in a game of football? They were too busy sweating it out to even care about their report card.

The Only Thing You Need to Know About Sports: It's Not About Winning

Forget the lessons on leadership, teamwork, and self-discipline that sports teach. The real takeaway here is that winning is everything, right? But don't let them lose a match at school, or suddenly they'll be the black sheep of the family. 'Beta, how could you lose the final match? Sharma ji's son would never!'

The Stereotypical 'Sports Kids' and the 'Real' Students
Oh, you know them—the sporty kids who somehow manage to excel at both scoring goals and scoring A+ marks. But of course, these kids are anomalies. What most parents seem to think is that if a child spends more than 30 minutes a day on the field, they'll forget how to spell their name. 'No, beta, you can't go play basketball. How will you ever solve this quadratic equation if you're busy making baskets?' Spoiler alert: It's called multitasking.

The Truth About Sports and Academic Performance
Here's the thing: studies show that physical activity actually boosts brain power. Shocking, right?

Playing basketball does more for your child's focus than any 10-hour revision session could ever achieve. But no, it's not nearly as glamorous as checking off 'studied for 12 hours' from the to-do list. The child who plays sports might actually understand concepts better, but who's got time for that? We've got exams to cram for!

The Real Cost of Ignoring Sports
So, here's what happens when we ignore sports and focus only on studying. Your child might become a math genius, but they'll likely miss out on crucial skills like teamwork, handling failure, and developing their social skills. You know, those things that are actually useful when

dealing with real-life challenges, like office politics or working with people who think 'teamwork' is just a buzzword.

The Health Boost: Why Sports Could Literally Save Your Life

Let's talk about health, shall we? Imagine this: you're not just running around the field for fun; you're also lowering your risk of heart disease, diabetes, and even cancer. Shocking, right?

Sports are like a one-stop shop for a healthier life. Kids who engage in physical activity regularly build stronger bones, muscles, and joints—something they'll thank themselves for when they're older.

In the future, when all the cramming for exams has long been forgotten, those few hours spent playing cricket or football will be the reason you're still able to run, jump, and live a full life. But, sure, keep skipping the sports, and when you're 40, you can try to outpace your health issues with a few extra hours of study. Spoiler alert: it doesn't work that way.

What Parents Can Do:

Here's a wild idea for you, parents: let your kids play. Yes, you read that right. Instead of turning every weekend into a 'study session', let them play a game of cricket or football. Don't worry, the world won't end because your child didn't spend the afternoon with a calculator. In fact, they might come out of it with better leadership skills and a sense of resilience that will help them tackle problems far more important than a missed exam question.

The Conclusion: It's Time to Rethink Sports

Look, I'm not saying sports should replace academics. But maybe, just maybe, they should stop being treated like the 'optional subject' that comes after hours. Kids need a balance—both in their minds and bodies. So, the next time your child asks to play, instead of immediately saying 'No, you need to study,' maybe try this: 'Sure, but let's also take a moment to talk about how challenges in sports teach us just as much as challenges in books.'

CHAPTER TWELVE

The Myth of the Perfect Teacher: What Makes a Great Educator?

Oh, here we go again. The myth that's been passed down from generation to generation: the idea of the "perfect teacher." You know, the one who never makes mistakes, has all the answers, and somehow manages to teach 30 kids, grade papers, prepare lessons, and still find time to sip tea without spilling a drop. Yeah, sure, that teacher exists in some magical land where unicorns teach math. But let's be real here: the truth is a bit messier.

> *"Let's break it down: **Teacher** + **Effort** = **Growth** (for both students and teachers)."*

And no, this equation doesn't mean your teacher should be a robot with a PhD and superhuman powers. It's time to stop expecting teachers to be walking, talking textbooks and start letting them be, you know, human.

"Superhuman expectations, zero support—let's bust the myth that teachers can do it all."

The "Perfect Teacher" Myth: It's Like Expecting the Perfect Pizza

The myth of the "perfect teacher" is like expecting the perfect pizza. Sure, it sounds great in theory, but even the best pizza has a few imperfections. I mean, have you ever tried one with pineapple on it? Some people love it, others... not so much. A teacher who admits they don't have all the answers? Now that's like the teacher version of adding extra cheese—delicious and real. But instead, we have this idea that teachers are supposed to be perfect calculators with perfect formulas, which is...well, kind of unrealistic, right?

So let's stop expecting teachers to be flawless and start encouraging them to be problem-solvers who are still learning and growing every day. Because guess what? The best teachers are those who can solve the equation of student success, even when the variables keep changing. They're not robots. They're people, and people make mistakes—just like we do. Shocking, I know.

<u>Why This Myth is Practically Wrong</u>

Teachers Are Not Machines

<u>Breaking news:</u> Teachers are not machines, and if you've ever tried to ask one to solve all your problems in five minutes, you'd know this firsthand. Teachers make mistakes, just like everyone else. In fact, the best teachers are the ones who admit their mistakes and show their students that errors are part of growth.

Imagine a teacher saying, "Whoops, I messed that up," and then walking you through how to fix it. That's real-life learning. But the myth of the perfect teacher? It's like asking them to perform a magic trick and then getting upset when the rabbit doesn't appear.

One Teacher Can't Have All the Answers

Here's a fun thought: Imagine if your teacher was supposed to have every single answer. Like, every single one. History, math, your weirdly specific questions about the meaning of life—yep, they should know it all.

So, next time you ask your teacher a question, remember: it's okay if they don't know everything. They're not there to recite facts like a living search engine. Instead, they're there to help guide you, ask questions, and help you figure out the answers. It's called teaching, not knowing everything.

Perfectionism is a Barrier to Growth

Let's get this straight: expecting teachers to be perfect is like expecting your dog to stop barking. It's just not going to happen. When we expect perfection from teachers, we stop them from being creative and trying new things. What happens when a teacher is afraid to try something new because they're worried about making a mistake? They play it safe. Boring, right? The best teachers are the ones who are constantly adapting and trying new things, not the ones pretending they have it all figured out.

The Role of Schools in Rethinking the "Perfect Teacher" Myth

Provide Ongoing Professional Development

Teachers need continuous development, not just one workshop a year that's so dry it could double as a sleep aid. Schools should offer teachers a chance to keep learning—yes, even teachers. This could be about the latest technology, classroom strategies, or how to deal with kids who believe they can magically "delete" their homework files. The point is: growth never stops.

Encourage Collaboration Over Isolation

You know what's great? Teachers working together. Sharing ideas, swapping horror stories about classroom chaos, and laughing about how no one really knows what a "flipped classroom" means. If schools would encourage collaboration rather than leaving teachers to fend for themselves, the results would be like a group project that actually works (shocking, I know). Teamwork makes the dream work, even for teachers.

Foster a Growth Mindset for Teachers

Just like we want students to have a growth mindset, teachers need it too. Schools should create an environment where teachers can experiment, fail, and learn from it. Imagine a world where teachers are not just perfect deliverers of knowledge, but learners too. Sounds like a place where everyone's growing, right?

What to Look for in Schools:
Don't be fooled by the "perfect teacher" myth. Sure, the teacher should be knowledgeable, but they should also know how to make learning engaging and fun. Look for a school where teachers are enthusiastic, approachable, and capable of making lessons interactive, not just dumping information. <u>A great teacher doesn't just lecture—they spark curiosity, make kids ask questions, and create an environment where students are excited to learn</u>. If the school's teaching is all about memorizing and following the rules, maybe it's time to move on to something a little more... engaging?

What Parents Can Do to Help at Home:
Parents, it's time to stop treating teachers like miracle workers. You're the first teacher your child ever had, so take some responsibility! Encourage curiosity at home, ask questions, and get your kids thinking about the world beyond their textbooks. Because guess what? Great teachers don't just deliver facts—they make kids think. And you should be doing the same.

Conclusion: Stop Worshipping Perfection
The myth of the "perfect teacher" is just that—a myth. Teachers aren't robots; they're human beings who are constantly learning and adapting. Let's stop setting unrealistic expectations and start supporting our teachers in their growth. After all, the best teachers aren't the ones who have all the answers; they're the ones who teach students how to find the answers themselves. So, next time you think about the "perfect teacher," maybe take a step

back and realize: imperfection is where the magic happens.

CHAPTER THIRTEEN

Your Kid is Not an Investment Plan

Middle-class parents often have one unspoken mantra: "<u>We struggled so you don't have to.</u>" It's a noble sentiment, but it often comes with strings attached—expectations that their children will excel in school, land prestigious jobs, and make their parents proud. The problem? These expectations often ignore what the child actually wants or is capable of. The result is a cycle of pressure, frustration, and disappointment on both sides. It's time to rethink whether we're raising children or ticking off a to-do list of societal approval.

"Kids need love, not ROI projections. Let's nurture their happiness, not just their report cards."

Why This Myth is Practically Wrong

1. Children Are Not Blank Slates

Parents often see their children as extensions of themselves, expecting them to fulfill dreams the parents couldn't achieve. But children come with their own personalities, interests, and abilities.

Example: A parent who always wanted to be a doctor might push their child into medicine, ignoring the fact that the child dreams of becoming a chef.

2. Expectations Can Be Unrealistic

Many parents expect their children to excel in academics, sports, music, and social skills—all at the same time. This "superchild" myth sets children up for failure and guilt when they inevitably fall short.

3. Comparison Culture

Comparing children to others ("Sharma ji's son scored 95%, why didn't you?") undermines their confidence and creates resentment. Every child develops at their own pace, and constant comparison only harms self-esteem.

4. Ignoring the Child's Interests

Expecting children to excel in fields they have no interest in leads to mediocrity at best and burnout at worst.

Example: A child forced into engineering despite loving writing may scrape through college but fail to build a fulfilling career.

Why Parents Need to Rethink This Practice

1. You're Raising a Person, Not a Trophy

The purpose of parenting isn't to create a "successful" child by society's standards—it's to nurture a happy, confident individual who can thrive in the world.

2. Your Struggles Are Not Their Burden

While middle-class families often work hard to provide better opportunities for their kids, it's unfair to expect children to repay that effort by following a specific path.

3. Expectations Lead to Pressure, Not Performance

A child under constant pressure to meet parental expectations may start associating their worth with achievements, leading to anxiety, stress, and even depression.

4. The World Has Changed

Success today doesn't look like it did 30 years ago. Fields like social media management, digital marketing, and graphic design didn't exist then but are now lucrative careers. Parents need to adapt their expectations to this evolving reality.

Examples of Why the Myth Fails

1. The Burnout Child:

A teenager juggling school, tuition, and extracurricular activities to meet their parents' expectations eventually loses interest in all of them, performing poorly across the board.

2. **The Silent Rebel:**

A child pushed into a career they dislike might go through the motions to please their parents but never put in the effort needed to truly succeed.

3. **The Career Switcher:**

Adults forced into "safe" careers often switch fields later in life, losing years of potential growth in their true passion.

<u>What Works Best Instead</u>

1. **Focus on Effort, Not Outcomes**

Praise your child for the effort they put in rather than the results they achieve. Example: "I'm proud of how much you studied for the test," rather than, "Why didn't you get 90%?"

2. **Encourage Exploration**

Let your child explore different interests without the pressure to excel immediately. Whether they try coding, baking, or football, the experience itself is valuable.

3. **Set Realistic Goals**

Understand your child's capabilities and set goals that challenge them without overwhelming them.

4. Celebrate Small Wins

Acknowledge progress, no matter how small. Example: If your child learns to play one song on the guitar, celebrate it rather than asking when they'll master the entire instrument.

5. Listen to Your Child

Ask your child what they enjoy and what they want to do. Open communication builds trust and ensures your expectations align with their dreams.

Supporting Evidence

1. Mental Health Research

- Studies show that children who feel supported rather than pressured by their parents are more likely to excel academically and emotionally.

2. Global Parenting Trends

- Northern European countries, known for their progressive education systems, prioritize child-led learning and holistic development over parental expectations.

3. **Success Stories**

   ○ Many successful individuals—like Steve Jobs, Oprah Winfrey, and P.V. Sindhu—pursued unconventional paths with the support of parents who encouraged their interests.

Why Unrealistic Expectations Hurt Kids

Experts like Dr. Suniya Luthar, a psychologist known for her research on adolescent development, emphasize that when parents place excessive expectations on their children, it can lead to stress, anxiety, and a fear of failure.

Dr. Luthar's studies show that kids who feel like they must "repay" their parents' sacrifices with academic or career success often experience burnout. Instead of pushing children to meet unrealistic standards, experts suggest that parents focus on supporting their kids in finding their own paths and understanding their strengths and passions.

Studies consistently show that children who grow up with high expectations from their parents are more likely to suffer from anxiety and depression. A study by the American Psychological Association found that children whose parents are overly critical or have high academic or career expectations are at an increased risk for mental health issues.

This evidence reinforces the idea that parents need to manage their expectations and avoid placing unrealistic pressure on their children to succeed in ways that don't align with their own desires and talents.

Conclusion

Dear parents, your child is not an extension of your unfulfilled dreams or a tool for social approval. They're individuals with their own paths to walk. Support them, guide them, and let them explore who they want to become.

After all, success isn't about meeting expectations—it's about finding happiness, fulfillment, and purpose. And hey, if they do become a stand-up comedian, at least you'll have free entertainment for family gatherings!

CHAPTER FOURTEEN

The Exam Season Apocalypse: Where Everyone's Life Depends on the Final Bell

Welcome to exam season—that glorious time of year when homes transform into full-scale war zones. The dining table becomes a battle map, textbooks are the weapons, and children are the reluctant foot soldiers marching toward academic glory. Parents, of course, assume the roles of generals, barking orders like:

"No TV until exams are over!"

"Why are you yawning? Drink chai and keep studying!"

"Sharma ji ka beta studies 10 hours a day—what's your excuse?"

"Does your child's 98% make you a better parent? Let's rethink this."

The war strategy is simple: all subjects, all chapters, and all marks must be conquered at any cost. Sleep is optional, snacks are carefully rationed, and free time? Don't even think about it. The family WhatsApp group suddenly becomes mission control, where every relative adds their "expert advice":

"Start with math, beta. Math is everything."

"Study from 4 AM—that's when the brain works best!"

"Take notes in blue pen. It boosts memory!"

The child, caught in the crossfire, stares at their textbooks like they're holding the answers to world peace. But the real villain? The Final Bell—the one that signals the end of the last exam, marking either celebration or disgrace (depending on whether you beat Sharma ji ka beta).

And let's not forget the silent drama:

- Mothers tiptoeing around the house like secret agents so as not to "disturb."
- Fathers scanning question banks like Sherlock Holmes.
- Neighbors dropping in "just to check" on how the child is "preparing." Spoiler alert: They're just there to compare and report back to headquarters.

But here's the punchline: The world outside? It doesn't care about the 98% your child scored in chemistry. No one asks whether you were Rank 1 before giving you a promotion or hiring you for a dream job. Yet, we treat these exams like life-or-death scenarios, forgetting that life itself has far bigger tests—tests that don't have guidebooks or question banks.

The Real Test: Life Doesn't Come with a Question Bank

Here's the thing—exams are not the final destination. They're just a pit stop in the race of life. No one will care whether you solved the toughest physics problem when you're negotiating your first salary. You'll never be asked, "Did you memorize all those formulas for success?"

Life isn't a multiple-choice quiz with a guaranteed answer. It's full of curveballs, and often, the real learning happens outside the exam room.

Yet, every exam season, we seem to forget this, turning the kitchen into a war room and the living room into an interrogation center. Why? Because we've been conditioned to believe that exams are the be-all and end-all. It's as if the world will only acknowledge our existence if we score a certain percentage. But guess what? It's just one tiny chapter in the story of a child's life.

What to Look for in Schools:

Does the school turn exam season into an apocalypse? If it feels like the end of the world when your child has exams, then something's wrong. Look for a school that teaches kids to prepare for exams without turning it into a life-or-death situation.

Exams should be a chance for students to show what they've learned, not an ordeal that makes everyone lose their minds. A good school will balance exam prep with self-care, ensuring students know how to manage stress and stay healthy during those high-pressure moments.

What Parents Can Do to Help at Home:

Parents, if you're treating exam season like a full-blown crisis, your child is going to pick up on that. Instead, keep calm, encourage balanced studying, and let them know that a test is just one part of their journey—not their entire future.

Help your child create a study schedule that balances work and breaks. Avoid the "you'll never get into a good college" speech and, instead, reassure them that they'll do their best, but it's not the end of the world if things don't go perfectly. Let them know that exams are just a small part of life—definitely not the thing that defines it.

Conclusion : Celebrating Effort, Not Just Results

So, dear parents and generals, maybe it's time to ease up. Celebrate effort, not just results. Encourage learning, not just memorization. And most importantly, remind kids that exams are a part of life—not the whole of it. Because when the dust settles after the exam season, what really matters is whether your child still enjoys learning, has confidence, and doesn't shudder every time someone says, "Beta, kitne marks aaye?"

In the end, the biggest test isn't the one written in textbooks or found in exam papers. It's the one your child faces when they walk into the real world—one where no amount of rote learning can prepare them for the unpredictability of life.

So, let's raise children who know that while exams are important, they're not everything. Life will test them in ways that no exam ever will. And as parents, our role is to help them see that there's more to life than marks—and that the real success is finding joy in learning, not just the fear of failure.

CHAPTER FIFTEEN

Schools: Factories of Toppers or Fields of Thinkers?

Schools have always played a crucial role in shaping a child's future, but sometimes, it feels like they're more focused on producing "toppers" than fostering creative thinkers. The myth is simple: "The more you memorize, the smarter you are." But let's break it down—

"Memorization ≠ True Learning."

The Problem with Memorization

"Are we molding minds to fit the system or nurturing them to shape the future?"

Schools often prioritize grades <u>because that's what parents demand</u>, not realizing they're stifling creativity in the process. Students end up memorizing facts for exams, only to forget them the moment the paper is submitted. While a solid foundation in subjects is necessary, education should go beyond rote learning. What if schools focused on nurturing problem-solvers and innovators instead of just chasing exam scores?

The Race for Results

Many schools proudly display their "100% pass rate" banners like they've just won the Olympics. But behind those banners are students cramming answers instead of understanding them. The focus is on results, not on the process of learning. Schools often prioritize grades because that's what parents demand, not realizing they're stifling creativity in the process.

> *"100% pass rate = 100% memorization, which often leads to 0% creativity.*
> *Now, let's flip the script: Creativity + Critical Thinking = Success + Innovation."*

Imagine if schools celebrated creativity the way they celebrate toppers. Instead of "Meet Alveena, 99% scorer in science," we could have, "Meet Alveena, who built a solar-powered fan for ₹200!" Imagine a world where problem-solving and innovation were just as celebrated as high exam scores. Now that's a story worth telling. It's not just about who gets the highest marks—it's about who is making the biggest impact!

Teaching vs. Coaching

The difference between a great school and a mediocre one? <u>A great school teaches children how to think, not what to think.</u> Unfortunately, many schools act as coaching centers, drilling formulas and definitions into young minds instead of fostering curiosity and deeper understanding.

> *"Here's the equation:*
> *Great School = Curiosity + Understanding*
> *Mediocre School = Memorization + Anxiety"*

A good teacher would ask, "Why do you think plants need sunlight?" and get kids to explore the answer. A rote-driven school might just say, "Memorize the photosynthesis equation by tomorrow." What would you prefer for your child? The tools to think critically, ask meaningful questions, and seek answers through exploration, or the ability to memorize for a test?

In a truly great school, the process of learning should excite the student. It should leave them thinking about questions long after the bell rings, hungry for answers, and motivated to understand the world in new ways.

Where's the Real-World Prep?

Many schools excel at preparing kids for exams but fail at preparing them for life. How about replacing one period of rote learning with lessons on teamwork, financial literacy, or even basic first aid?

When was the last time your child's school taught them how to cook a meal, balance a budget, or even just say "no" politely? These are the lessons they'll carry forever—not how to calculate the square root of 144. While math is important, it should be part of a broader education that teaches life skills.

> "*Real-Life Prep = Teamwork + Financial Literacy + Cooking + Communication*
> *Exam Prep = Algebra + Trigonometry + Memorization*"

Let's equip our kids for the real world, not just for exams. Imagine a school curriculum that blends both, like Math + Life Skills = The Best of Both Worlds! This way, students don't just get ready for an exam—they get ready for life.

Incorporating real-world skills would mean schools focus on preparing students to succeed in the future, not just the next exam. Teamwork, time management, emotional intelligence—these are the skills that will shape the leaders of tomorrow. So why not start teaching them today?

Learning Beyond the Classroom

It's not just about sitting in a classroom for hours; true learning happens when students can connect their education to the world around them. Schools should be places where students engage with real-world problems, collaborate with others, and think about how they can contribute to society.

Field trips, internships, creative projects, and hands-on experiences should be part of the learning process. Imagine if, instead of just learning about history in textbooks, students took part in reenacting important events, or if math lessons included budgeting for a class project. These practical applications of knowledge make learning more engaging and give students a sense of purpose.

The Ultimate Goal: Lifelong Learners

At the end of the day, what's the goal of education? It's not just about preparing students to ace their exams. It's about preparing them to succeed in life—about giving them the tools to adapt, think critically, solve problems, and innovate.

Success in life doesn't come from memorizing formulas and passing tests. It comes from the ability to apply knowledge creatively, think critically, and continuously learn. Schools should focus on helping students develop these skills, so they are equipped to tackle any challenge that comes their way.

Conclusion

Schools have the potential to be fertile fields where ideas bloom, not factories churning out identical report cards. It's time for schools to redefine success—not by the number of toppers they produce but by the number of thinkers, creators, and problem-solvers they nurture.

So, dear schools, let's shift the focus from "<u>Who got the highest marks</u>?" to "<u>Who asked the most interesting question today</u>?" Because, as any good math teacher would tell you, sometimes the question is more important than the answer! Let's focus on building curious minds, not just test-takers. After all, the future needs thinkers, not memorizers.

CHAPTER SIXTEEN

Doctor, Engineer, or Disappointment?

In middle-class India, career options seem to come preloaded: you're either a doctor, an engineer, or that "other" category whispered at family gathering. Parents who struggle to pay private school fees often see STEM careers as the golden ticket to stability, ignoring the fact that arts, humanities, or careers in commerce can be equally rewarding. But here's the truth: the world doesn't need just engineers; it needs storytellers, designers, social workers, and yes, marketers who can actually sell stuff.

"Two choices, zero imagination. What about the road less traveled?"

Why This Myth is Practically Wrong

STEM Doesn't Guarantee Success

- Just because your child becomes an engineer doesn't mean they'll invent the next WhatsApp. In fact, many engineers end up in unrelated jobs like sales or customer support. Why? Because the field is overcrowded, and not everyone is passionate about it.
- Imagine: a software engineer who hates coding but took the job because "log kya kahenge" (what will

people say).

Arts and Humanities Aren't "Backup Plans"

Careers in fields like journalism, design, psychology, and marketing can be just as lucrative and fulfilling. A clinical psychologist earning ₹1 lakh a month is no less successful than an engineer doing the same. The difference? The psychologist is genuinely passionate about helping people understand and improve their mental well-being.

Creativity is the New Currency

The job market is changing. Employers now value creativity, emotional intelligence, and communication skills over technical degrees.

For example, a UX designer who combines creativity and technical skills is in high demand, even without an engineering degree.

Pigeonholing Kills Potential

Forcing your child into STEM may make them resentful. Instead of becoming a happy engineer, they might end up as a frustrated adult reminiscing about their "lost art dreams."

Why Parents Need to Rethink This Practice

Middle-Class Families Can't Afford to Gamble on Passionless Careers

Engineering and medical studies are expensive. If your child isn't passionate, you're not just wasting money; you're setting them up for failure or mediocrity.

It's better to let them shine in a field they love than force them into one they hate.

Your Neighbor's Child is Not a Benchmark

"Sharma ji ka beta" is a mythological creature used to guilt-trip middle-class kids. Just because their child is in IIT doesn't mean yours has to follow. Maybe your child has a different gift—writing, designing, or even marketing products better than Sharma ji ka beta can code them.

Jobs in Marketing and Office Work Are Real Jobs

A common misconception is that "office jobs" like HR, PR, or marketing aren't prestigious. But guess what? These professionals keep companies running, earn good salaries, and often enjoy better work-life balance than engineers coding till midnight.

The Future is Interdisciplinary

The future isn't about STEM vs. arts; it's about combining them. Fields like animation, game design, and digital marketing blend creativity with technology, offering exciting and well-paying opportunities.

What Works Best Instead

1. Let Kids Explore

Allow your child to experiment with different fields. If they like numbers, let them try accounting, economics, or even marketing analytics. If they love drawing, introduce them to fields like UX/UI design or advertising.

2. Encourage Practical Experience

Internships, workshops, and projects help children understand what a career actually entails. For example, a child interested in marketing could help a local shop design posters or manage their social media.

3. **Combine Fields**

Encourage careers that blend STEM and arts. For example:
Animation (combines technology and creativity)
Marketing analytics (combines math and communication)
Environmental policy (combines science and humanities)

Focus on Soft Skills
Whether your child becomes a marketer, engineer, or office administrator, skills like communication, teamwork, and problem-solving will always be in demand.

Expert Opinions: Why Pushing Kids Into Certain Careers Is Harmful
Experts like Dr. Shyamala Gopinath, a career psychologist, argue that pushing children into traditional career paths—like medicine or engineering—can lead to resentment and a lack of fulfillment. Dr. Gopinath suggests that children should be encouraged to explore careers based on their strengths and passions. She stresses that every child is unique, and their future career satisfaction depends on discovering a path that aligns with their interests and talents.

What to Look for in Schools:

Does the school push your child toward being a doctor, engineer, or... well, a failure? It's time to find a school that promotes a wide range of career options. A good school helps students discover their interests and strengths—not just push them toward a narrow set of "prestigious" careers.

Whether your child wants to be a teacher, artist, entrepreneur, or scientist, the school should support their dreams. Look for a place that values diversity in career paths and encourages exploration.

Supporting Evidence: The Need for Career Exploration

Studies from the National Career Development Association (NCDA) show that children who are exposed to a wide range of career options from an early age tend to be more satisfied with their career choices later in life. Early exploration allows students to find what truly excites them, leading to higher levels of motivation and success. This highlights the importance of not forcing children into careers they're not passionate about, but instead giving them the space to explore their interests.

Conclusion: A Better Way Forward

It's time to stop treating career choices as a one-size-fits-all decision. Instead of pushing kids into specific career paths, let's help them explore their interests and strengths. Whether they end up in a traditional profession like medicine or engineering, or pursue something creative like design or filmmaking, the key is to support them in finding a career that excites them. A future where children are empowered to choose careers based on their passions will create happier, more fulfilled adults.

Echoes of My Journey

Back in school, choosing a stream after 10th was nothing short of a dramatic Bollywood climax. While some students got to pick their own path, others had their futures decided for them by parents and societal expectations. "Beta, science le lo. Doctor ya engineer ban jaoge!" It didn't matter if their math scores were crying for help or if they thought Newton was a brand of fruit.

I watched in amusement as many of my friends, who struggled to pass science, bravely marched into the science stream. It was as if choosing science would magically turn them into Einstein overnight. Meanwhile, the lucky ones who had a say in their futures happily opted for commerce or arts.

Fast forward 10 years. The commerce grads are out there thriving, with steady jobs, good salaries, and a balanced work-life. You'll find them buying cars, posting vacation pictures on Instagram, and generally enjoying life. And the forceful entrants into science? Many struggled to complete their degrees, while others are still figuring out where life went off track.

A note to everyone: Those who chose science out of genuine passion have gone on to achieve great success. But for those who entered science under pressure or societal expectations, the journey has been far more difficult.

So, to all the parents out there dreaming of raising doctors and engineers, take a moment to ask your child: "Are you passionate about science, or are you just trying to please the family WhatsApp group?"

And to the students: Choose science only if you love it, not because everyone else is doing it. After all, it's better to excel in commerce or arts than to struggle in a field you never wanted to be in!

———————

CHAPTER SEVENTEEN

The Coaching Center Myth: Is It Just a Money-Making Machine?

Alright, let's talk about the shiny, glittery world of coaching centers and tuition classes. You know, those places that promise to turn your kid into a genius overnight and get them into the "top colleges" (you know the ones, the ones with a reputation for sending kids to places with the highest pressure and lowest sleep).

If you're a middle-class parent, you're probably already familiar with the drill: You spend half your paycheck on tuition, your child spends all their time cramming, and at the end of the day, everyone's tired, stressed, and no one's actually sure what they learned. But hey, at least you got a certificate of completion, right?

Competitive exams are one path to success, not the *only* path.

The Syllabus is the Same—Why the Separate Coaching Biz?

Here's a fun fact: The syllabus for board exams and competitive exams like NEET and JEE is essentially the same. Yes, you read that right. The difference? One has a much more expensive price tag attached to it. The concepts are the same. The formulas are the same. The only thing that changes is the level of stress—and the fees for "advanced" coaching.

But let's keep pretending that the only way to succeed is by drowning our kids in extra hours of study. Does anyone else see the irony? We've been sold this idea that our children need to prepare separately for exams that cover basically the same material. Welcome to the coaching center hustle!

Understanding Concepts Is the Key—And Guess What? No Extra Coaching Needed!

Here's the mind-blowing truth: If kids actually understood the concepts from the start—in their lower grades—they wouldn't need to waste money on coaching centers that are just repeating the same material over and over.

Understanding the basics is key. Yet, we're spending more time making our kids memorize formulas and equations, than actually understanding why those formulas even exist. You know, those annoying "why" questions?

But hey, who needs to understand when we can just pay for the magic "shortcut" in the form of coaching, right? If only life worked that way, we'd all just pay for shortcuts and skip the whole "effort" part. So why not invest in building strong foundations early?

If kids had a solid grasp of the basics in elementary school, they'd cruise through middle school and high school, without needing special classes in every subject. But no, we're too busy handing over our wallets to coaching centers.

Alternatives to the Costly-Coaching Center

Now, here's the fun part. You don't need to spend a fortune on these overpriced classes. Let's think of some alternatives that don't require you to sell your kidneys to pay for them:

<u>Online Resources:</u> There are tons of free and affordable resources online that cover every topic your child will need. Whether it's Khan Academy, YouTube, or free online textbooks, there's no reason to pay for "extra" classes.

<u>Private Tutors:</u> Instead of sending your child to a big, fancy coaching center, hire a private tutor who can focus on the areas where your child is struggling. You get personalized attention without the price tag of a corporate coaching center.

<u>Group Study:</u> Encourage your child to form study groups with friends. No, this isn't the same as "cramming"

together—it's about sharing knowledge, helping each other, and learning in a stress-free environment. Plus, it's free!

<u>Encourage Independent Learning:</u> The best way to learn is by actively solving problems. Provide your child with practice tests, encourage reading, and let them learn through doing. Trust me, the results will surprise you.

Conclusion: Let's Stop Feeding the Coaching Center Machine

The bottom line? Coaching centers aren't the magic solution to your child's future success—they're a business, and you're just another customer. Instead of treating them like a necessity, let's focus on building a strong foundation, nurturing curiosity, and teaching our children to truly understand what they're learning. Let's stop spending money on shortcuts and focus on giving our kids the skills they need to succeed—whether they're studying for a board exam or learning to bake their first cake.

So, next time you're asked, "Should I sign up for the special coaching class?" just ask yourself: "Is my child learning, or are they just paying for a fancy certificate of 'success'?"

Echoes of My Journey

During my 12th standard in a government school, something magical happened—our physics, chemistry, and math lecturers suddenly started showing extraordinary care for us. Their concern for our future blossomed into... paid tuitions! Out of 34 students in my class, 32 dutifully enrolled in these "career-saving" tuitions. And then there were the remaining two rebels: me and another poor soul who apparently missed the memo.

The real fun began in the classroom. Take physics, for instance—our teacher would confidently solve half a derivation on the board, then pause dramatically, as if building suspense for a movie climax. "We'll finish the rest in tuition," he'd say, leaving the two of us staring blankly, wondering if we were part of some exclusive non-premium plan.

As the months went by, I learned two important lessons:

1. Gravity pulls everything down—especially my marks.

2. The coaching business is a goldmine, but only if you're the one collecting fees.

Needless to say, my career aspirations took a nosedive, thanks to a system where education turned into a subscription service. Since then, my feelings toward the coaching industry have been simple and eternal: "Thanks, but no thanks!"

On a brighter note, this experience did teach me something valuable—education should never be about profit. It should be about empowerment, and no child should be made to feel like their future is on hold unless they pay for the "full version" of learning.

CHAPTER EIGHTEEN

Math for Boys, Art for Girls? Breaking the Pink and Blue Divide

"Boys are better at math," "Girls shouldn't play rough sports," or "This career isn't for women"—these are phrases middle-class parents hear and, unfortunately, sometimes believe. Gender stereotypes have long dictated what children can study, which hobbies they pursue, and what careers they're "allowed" to consider. But here's the reality: Brains don't have genders. The idea that certain fields or skills are reserved for one gender isn't just outdated—it's outright wrong.

"Talents don't have genders. Let's rewrite the rules and shatter the stereotypes."

<u>**Why This Myth is Practically Wrong**</u>

1. Science Doesn't Support It

Research consistently shows no inherent difference in abilities between boys and girls in fields like math, science, or sports. Any differences are societal, not biological.

Example: Girls often outperform boys in STEM subjects in countries that actively combat stereotypes, like Finland and Sweden.

2. Limits Potential

Gender stereotypes discourage kids from exploring their interests and talents, leading to missed opportunities and unfulfilled potential.

Example: A boy interested in cooking might avoid pursuing it as a career due to societal judgment, even though top chefs like Sanjeev Kapoor dominate the field.

3. The Modern Job Market is Gender-Neutral

Careers in coding, design, healthcare and sales, don't require a specific gender. What they need are skills, passion, and creativity.

4. Stereotypes Harm Both Genders

Girls are told to be nurturing, steering them toward "soft" careers like teaching or nursing, while boys are pressured to be aggressive and competitive, limiting their ability to express emotions or pursue creative fields.

Why Parents Need to Rethink This Practice

1. Your Child's Future Doesn't Need Gender Labels

Whether your daughter wants to be a robotics engineer or your son dreams of being a fashion designer, their career paths shouldn't be dictated by societal norms.

2. The World is Changing

Women are excelling in fields traditionally dominated by men, like engineering, finance, and space exploration, while men are thriving in creative and caregiving roles.

Example: Indian women like Kalpana Chawla (astronaut) and Gita Gopinath (economist) have shattered stereotypes on a global scale.

3. Stereotypes Hurt Boys Too

Boys are often discouraged from pursuing careers like teaching, nursing, or dance, even though these fields are just as valuable and rewarding.

Example: A male primary school teacher can bring unique perspectives to nurturing and educating young children.

4. Diverse Teams Outperform

Research shows that gender-diverse teams are more innovative and productive, proving that breaking stereotypes benefits everyone, not just individuals.

<u>Examples of Why the Myth Fails</u>

1. The "Good Girl" Trap:

A girl who's excellent at math is discouraged from pursuing engineering because "it's a tough career for women," leading her to settle for a less challenging field.

2. **The "Tough Guy" Burden:**

A boy who loves painting is mocked for choosing "girly" hobbies, pushing him to give up his passion for fear of judgment.

3. **Missed Opportunities:**

A parent steers their daughter away from sports because "it's not ladylike," missing out on the possibility of her becoming the next Sania Mirza or PV Sindhu.

What Works Best Instead

1. **Encourage Exploration Regardless of Gender**

Let kids explore their interests, whether it's coding, dance, or football, without worrying about societal norms.

2. **Celebrate Role Models**

Highlight real-life role models who've broken stereotypes:

- **Women:** Mary Kom (boxing), Sudha Murthy (engineering, philanthropy).
- **Men:** Vikas Khanna (chef), Prabhu Deva (dancer).

3. Challenge Stereotypes at Home

Avoid gendered language and expectations at home. For example:

- Instead of "Girls shouldn't climb trees," say, "Be careful while climbing."
- Instead of "Boys don't cry," say, "It's okay to feel upset."

4. Introduce Diverse Activities

Enroll children in diverse activities that break gender norms: martial arts for girls, cooking or art for boys.

5. Support Career Choices

If your child expresses interest in a nontraditional career, support them wholeheartedly. A girl who wants to be a pilot or a boy who dreams of being a writer needs encouragement, not skepticism.

Supporting Evidence

1. Historical Examples

Rani Lakshmibai led armies, challenging the notion that leadership is a male trait. Similarly, Raja Ravi Varma's artwork proves men can excel in creative fields.

2. Research on Gender Stereotypes

Studies reveal that children exposed to gender-neutral environments perform better in a wider range of activities and show greater career ambition.

Conclusion

Dear parents, your child's potential isn't limited by their gender—it's limited by societal stereotypes. By encouraging your children to explore their interests without worrying about labels, you're not just raising boys or girls; you're raising confident, capable individuals. Let them dream, let them fail, and let them succeed in whatever path they choose—whether it's piloting planes, designing dresses, or playing the drums. After all, the world doesn't need more stereotypes; it needs more trailblazers.

CHAPTER NINETEEN

Failure is Not the End: It's the Beginning of Something Great

Failure—the word that sends a shiver down the spine of students, parents, and teachers alike. In the Indian education system, failure is like the villain in every Bollywood movie—always hiding in the background, always feared, and somehow always the one thing you're not allowed to experience.

Parents treat failure like it's a natural disaster, while students will do anything to avoid it—whether it's copying assignments or pretending they understand calculus when all they really know is how to hide a textbook. Schools, of course, jump right on the bandwagon, creating a space where failure is treated like an actual crime.

But here's the truth: failure isn't some form of punishment—it's the universe's way of saying, "Hey, you're so close. Just a little more effort and I'll let you in on the secret to success." Failure is like that annoying but necessary pit stop on the road to greatness. So, relax! If you're failing, congratulations—you're officially learning!

"Grades can fall, but resilience rises. Every failure teaches something new."

"Let's break it down with a little math:
Failure = Learning Opportunity + Growth
But wait, **Fear of Failure = Stress + Missed Opportunities + One Big Mess of Nervous Energy.**

So, let's stop treating failure like it's the final exam of life. Instead, let's start treating it like a "pop quiz" for success!

Why This Myth is Wrong

1. Failure is Not a Dead End

Ah, the classic panic mode: "I failed. It's over. My life is ruined. I might as well just drop out and become a street artist." Sound familiar? Well, here's the thing: failure is **not** the end of your story. It's just a chapter, a **plot twist**—one that makes the story more interesting.

Think of failure like your favorite movie villain who *almost* wins but gets defeated in the end. Without failure, we wouldn't have success stories, we'd just have... "meh" stories. So, take a deep breath. Your academic career (and life in general) isn't going to be over because you didn't ace that one test.

2. The Perfect Student Myth

Schools often glorify "perfect students" who never fail and always top the class. The reality is, these students are probably terrified of making a mistake, and let's be honest, perfection is overrated. The truth is, the students who fail, **try**, and fail again are often the ones who learn the most. So, why are we putting such a high pedestal on the "perfect student" when they're probably living in constant fear of failure, unable to explore their full potential?

> "*The best students are not the ones who avoid failure—they're the ones who embrace it, learn from it, and come back stronger.*"

3. Fear of Failure = Missed Opportunities

Here's the kicker: when you're so terrified of failing, you'll probably avoid trying new things altogether. The fear of failure is like a prison. If you stay locked up in your safe little bubble of "I'm going to play it safe," you'll never grow, learn, or achieve anything truly remarkable. Guess what? You can't be amazing without failing a few times. That's like trying to bake a cake without breaking an egg. It just doesn't work.

Better Solutions: Embrace Failure Like a Boss

Celebrate Mistakes

Instead of hiding your failures, why not **celebrate** them? The more you fail, the more you learn. And the more you learn, the more confident you become. If you never fail, you're probably not trying hard enough.

Imagine telling your friends, "I got a question wrong in class today. It was AWESOME!" Sounds ridiculous, right? But imagine if schools had a "Mistake Wall" where students could proudly showcase their failures and what they learned from them. It would be the "Wall of Fame" for future problem solvers.

Normalize Failure in Schools

Schools need to take a page from the "Fail Forward" philosophy. Instead of punishing students for making mistakes, encourage them to analyze what went wrong and learn from it.

Schools should hold **Failure Day**, where everyone shares one thing they've tried and failed at, and what they learned. This would not only normalize failure but also foster a growth mindset where the goal is progress, not perfection.

Redefine Success

Success is not about never failing; it's about failing and getting back up. Instead of measuring success by grades alone, let's measure it by **growth**. How much did you learn? How much did you grow? How many new things did you try?

Let's not pretend that getting 100% in a test is the only thing that matters. The real world doesn't care about your grades—it cares about whether you can apply what you know to solve real problems. And guess what? You can't solve problems without facing a few failures along the way.

Develop a "Growth Mindset"

Here's a secret: every time you fail, you get a little bit smarter, a little bit more experienced. **Growth Mindset** is all about understanding that your abilities aren't fixed—they grow as you try, fail, learn, and try again. It's about knowing that failure is temporary, and it doesn't define you.

The more you embrace challenges and learn from them, the more resilient you become. It's like building muscles in the gym—without the sweat, pain, and occasional "I can't feel my legs" moments, you'll never grow stronger.

Conclusion

It's time to stop fearing failure and start **celebrating** it. Failure isn't a monster under your bed, it's the teacher who's trying to help you grow. So, the next time you fail, don't cry into your textbooks. Stand tall, learn from it, and share your story of resilience with the world.

Remember, failure is just the universe's way of giving you a little nudge in the right direction. So let's embrace it, learn from it, and move forward. After all, every great success story started with a failure or two!

CHAPTER TWENTY

Let's Rethink Everything, Shall We?

So, what have we really learned in this mind-bending, myth-busting journey through the Great Indian Education System?

Let's break it down: marks don't equal success, rote learning is a ticket to nowhere, and obsessing over exams is a surefire way to raise stressed-out robots instead of curious, capable humans.

Oh, and don't even get me started on the coaching centers—they're like that overpriced magic potion that promises success but only gives you a headache and an empty wallet.

But let's be real—none of this is really new, is it?

Parents, you've been running in this marathon, thinking the finish line is just around the corner. But every time you think you're close, you end up in a new starting line.

Teachers, you've been drowning in paperwork, lesson plans, and students who are only interested in the marks, not the learning.

And **students?** Well, you've been doing your best to survive the endless cycle of exams, assignments, and a pressure cooker of expectations. Everyone's trying to win the race, but no one really knows where the race is headed.

Here's a crazy thought—what if it's all nonsense? What if everything you've been told about exams, grades, and competition is just... well, the world's longest, most tiring con job?

What if success has nothing to do with how much you memorize, and everything to do with how much you understand?

Imagine a world where education is about curiosity, creativity, and critical thinking—not memorization, standardized testing, and suffocating competition. A world where failure isn't the end of the world but the start of a journey. Where students can learn at their own pace, teachers have the freedom to teach beyond the textbook, and parents stop treating their kids like personal projects that need to be "perfected."

And just when you think you've cracked it, here's the twist: You don't have to **"crack"** anything. You just have to **understand**.

Now, here's the fun part: You've read all this. You've probably nodded in agreement. You might even feel like you've had an enlightenment. You're thinking, Yes! Understanding is the key. Forget the grades. Let's focus on real learning!

And here's where the plot twist happens. After reading this entire book—after all the sarcasm, all the reality checks, all the mind-bending insights, 98% of you will still go back to the same old routine.

That's right. You'll go back to stressing over marks, pushing your child to memorize 20 pages in one night, and signing up for coaching classes that promise the world but deliver little more than stress-induced hair loss.

Why? Because it's easier. It's familiar. It's what everyone else is doing, and we've all been conditioned to believe that success is measured by how many formulas you can recite, how many problems you can solve under pressure, and how many coaching classes you can afford. We've bought into the idea that memorization is the only path to success.

Only 2% of you will actually take the time to rethink the entire system. You'll realize that real learning doesn't come from copying a thousand pages from a book. It comes from understanding. It comes from engaging with ideas, experimenting, failing, and then getting up to try again. The other 98% will continue chasing the same old cycle, but at least the 2% will know the truth—*Marks are Just Numbers*.

What If..?

The **"What If"** section takes a funny, imaginative twist on the myths we've all grown up believing—those that dominate the Indian education system. It's where logic meets absurdity, and you get a moment to laugh at how we sometimes take marks, exams, and systems way too seriously. These "what if" scenarios will challenge readers to reflect while enjoying a bit of comic relief.

1. What If... Marks Really Measured Talent?

Imagine a world where marks aren't given for answers but for talents.

- Your child paints a sunset? *"Beta, 95/100! Perfect brush strokes!"*
- Your neighbor's kid can hit a cricket ball over the wall? *"Wow! 98%! Strong sixer skills!"*
- The kid who fixes the leaking tap at home? *"Topper! Practical skills: 100/100!"*

Suddenly, parent-teacher meetings would look like talent auditions, and question papers would ask: *"Draw your favorite animal"* or *"Cook a dish in under 10 minutes"*. Kids wouldn't fear exams—they'd show off their skills with pride.

Takeaway:
Marks measure how well you write answers, not how talented or capable you are in real life. Let's celebrate every child's unique skills—because life needs more chefs, artists, and thinkers, not just rank holders.

2. What If... Coaching Centers Guaranteed Success?

Imagine coaching centers worked like magic factories—drop in your kid, and *"ding!"* out pops a future CEO, doctor, or IITian.

- Students would leave class holding golden trophies saying *"Guaranteed Future Success"*.
- Parents would collect their kids like shiny new products off an assembly line.
- Coaching center owners? Millionaires, of course—smiling like they've solved world hunger.

But here's the catch: In this magical world, everyone would be the *same*—all doctors, all engineers, all toppers. No dreamers, no writers, no artists. How boring would that be?

Takeaway:

Success isn't factory-made, and coaching can't replace curiosity, hard work, or passion. Real success comes when children follow their dreams, not just a syllabus.

3. What If... Exams Were Open-Book and Open-Internet?

Imagine exams where students were told, *"Google the answer if you like. Use your books. Just show us how you solve it!"*

- No panic, no memorization. Students would focus on understanding *how* to find answers, not on remembering random facts.
- A history paper would ask, *"How would you prevent World War II if you were the leader?"*
- A math exam would say, *"Solve this problem any way you*

like—show your reasoning!"

Suddenly, exams wouldn't be about cramming. They'd be about thinking, exploring, and problem-solving—skills that actually matter.

Takeaway:
In the real world, no one stops you from looking up answers. What matters is knowing *how* to think, research, and solve problems—not how much you can memorize.

4. What If... Failing an Exam Earned You a Prize?

Imagine failing an exam didn't mean shame and punishment. Instead, it meant you got a *prize*—a chance to explore what you really love.

- Failed math? Congratulations! You get a free art class to discover your creativity.
- Flunked science? Great! Here's a pass to the sports ground to find your inner athlete.

Parents would proudly say, *"My child failed the physics test but discovered he's an amazing chess player!"* Failure wouldn't be the end—it would be the start of something new and exciting.

Takeaway:
Failure is not the opposite of success; it's a step toward it. Every failure teaches something important—let's stop fearing it and start learning from it.

5. What If... Schools Taught Real-Life Skills?

Imagine schools teaching things that kids will actually use in life.

- Instead of writing a 5-page essay on *"The Importance of Time,"* kids would learn how to plan their day with calendars and reminders.
- Instead of memorizing the periodic table, students would learn how to fix a leaking tap or file taxes.
- Exams would test, *"Can you cook a basic meal without burning the kitchen?"* or *"Draft an email to your boss explaining a mistake."*

Students would leave school ready to *live*, not just to score marks. No more adults staring at flat tyres, broken sinks, or bank statements like they're alien puzzles.

Takeaway:
Real life is the final exam. It's time we teach skills that help kids survive—and thrive—beyond the classroom.

6. What If... Parents Got Report Cards Too?

Imagine if parents were graded on how well they supported their kids during exam season.

- **Communication**: Did you say, *"Do your best!"* or *"Sharma ji ka beta got 98%, and you?"*
- **Patience**: Did you give your child breathing space, or did you hover like a helicopter with a stopwatch?
- **Encouragement**: Did you celebrate effort or cry over 2 lost marks?

At the end of exam season, kids would proudly hand their parents a report card: *"Mom: A+ for being kind and supportive. Dad: B for too many chai breaks!"*

Takeaway:
Exams aren't just tough for kids—they're a test for parents too. Support, love, and patience matter more than marks.

Final Note:

The "What If" section isn't just about making you laugh—it's about imagining a better way to approach education. Because sometimes, the most absurd questions are the ones that make us think the hardest.

What if we focused less on marks and more on learning? What if failure wasn't the end but a new beginning? What if every child had the freedom to explore, question, and create?

Now that's a world worth imagining.